Michigan
Triumphs and Tragedies
Vol. 1

By Dale Killingbeck
RER Publishing
Tustin, Michigan 49688

I

First Printing, February 2005

Copyright ©2005 by Dale Killingbeck
All rights reserved.

ISBN 0-9762758-0-5

CHAPTERS

I give thanks to the Lord Jesus Christ who gave the state of Michigan its beauty and resources.

This book is dedicated to my wife, Mindy, and our eight beautiful children who allowed me the time to research and write this book. I also want to thank Mark Jager for his encouragement and for help at Clarke Historical Library at Central Michigan University and Michigan Technological University's historical library staff for their help.

Bradley Looy gets great thanks for his technical assistance and cover design.

-- Dale Killingbeck, October 2004

Introduction

This book is written for all those who think Michigan history is boring.

It's not. I challenge you to read the stories contained between the covers of this book and tell me you were bored.

Michigan's history boasts personality, perseverance and tragedy. Truly, fact sometimes is stranger than fiction -- and far more interesting.

Our state's past involves land and water and the people who rowed and dug and created a state through hardship, sweat, muscle and dogged determination.

The traders and Indians, pioneer farmers and lumberjacks, the railroad men and the miners, the sailors and just plain adventurers all leave rich and fascinating stories as valuable as any chunk of ore or log of white pine.

The purpose of this book is to tap into that richness and glean gems from the lives and sacrifices of those who endured hardship and disaster and troubles and trials and in the end overcame.

Some of these stories are about disaster, some about daring feats, others about endurance, but all are related in some way to this state's great history. There are stories the reader may know of but never really bothered to understand, and there are names that are familiar, but they may not be known in the setting depicted within these pages.

There are hundreds of people and stories worthy of our remembrance and this endeavor, prayerfully, is just the beginning as we consider the triumphs and tragedies of lives that have gone before us.

In the context of modern day Michigan, we are blessed to live in a rich state and reap from the efforts of all those who have sown before us.

Chapter One:
Daniel Boone and Detroit

During the struggle against the British in America's great war of independence, what is now Michigan remained the frontier.

Although the French in the late 1600s claimed the territory for their king, the British successfully later took away that claim in the French and Indian War of 1754 to 1763. And as the two powers operated in the land of the great inland waters, neither the British nor the French pushed any settlement of the land. After winning the war against the French, Britain's Royal Proclamation of 1763 forbid any white settlement beyond the Allegheny Mountains.

Michigan forests, rivers and swamps proved too valuable for

1

the fur trade and many Indian tribes remained within what is now the Midwest and would have to be negotiated with before any settlements could successfully be established.

As the American Revolution unfolded in Boston and the blood was shed at Lexington and Concord – the British strategy in the West became containment. The Declaration of Independence was signed in 1776 and war broke out in the East, America's focus turned to the need to help General George Washington mobilize an army. Beyond the Allegheny Mountains and across what is now Ohio to Detroit and down across the Ohio Valley and into what became Kentucky, the British aimed to remove any roots of American rebellion sown into the soil.

In 1769, Daniel Boone and some other pioneer settlers from North Carolina entered the region that is now Kentucky against the British law. A North Carolina land speculator made a deal with the Cherokee nation for land and Boone led the way as his agent into the uncharted interior. Within a few years he established a settlement at Boonesborough on the Kentucky River, just southeast of where Lexington, Kentucky is today.

Boonesborough along with other small settlements in Kentucky and Ohio became targets for raids by Indians led by British or French operatives.

As the war unfolded, Detroit became a center for Indian guerilla fighters and its civil leader, Lt. Governor Henry Hamilton, quickly established a reputation among the Americans for his policy of ordering Indian raids and paying the warriors for the scalps they brought back.

Many settlers called Hamilton the "Hair Buyer."

The British official first arrived in Detroit in November 1775 and began repairing and strengthening defenses for the village. At that time Detroit consisted of about 2 acres of land and was surrounded by a stockade of maple saplings dug into the ground. The saplings rose about 12 feet into the air – preventing any flying leaps inside.

There was not any fort, just a citadel used as a parade ground and barracks for soldiers. It sat on Jefferson Avenue and Wayne Street.

About 1,500 whites were protected by a garrison of two companies of the King's Eighth Regiment. As Hamilton surveyed the situation, he ordered the soldiers to strengthen fortifications by building a ditch around the stockade. They also constructed new blockhouses and batteries.

Hamilton also went to work trying to woo Indians to the British side of the coming conflict, just as American ambassadors were at work on the other side. Tribes in the region included the Ottawas, Chippewas, Wyandottes, Shawnees, Senecas, Delewares, Cherokees and Potawatomies. Hamilton was successful in neutralizing any influence the Americans had on the tribes.

In August 1776, Hamilton received a visit from two Indian messengers sent from Virginia to Indian tribes in the region. Captain White Eyes, a Deleware chief, and Mountons, a Virginia-educated Indian, carried a letter and special Indian belts asking the Western Indians to meet at a conference in what is now Pittsburgh. Hamilton took the letter and cut the belts in front of all the Indians assembled. He then sent the pair out of the settlement.

Before they left, a copy of the Pennsylvania Gazette of July 24, 1776, was produced. It included a copy of the Declaration of Independence. Hamilton and the rest of Detroit learned about the new nation.

As the war unfolded, Hamilton regularly sent out raiding parties of Indians and whites to attack settlers and settlements. Among the settlements in their sights was Boonesborough.

Daniel Boone at that time was a captain in the militia, he would later become a colonel. He fought in a handful of battles during the revolution. But he remained more a frontiersman than soldier.

During the winter of 1778, he and others from his settlement went to the Blue Licks on the Licking River in Kentucky to get salt. Salt in those days was a precious commodity for preserving meat and other foods.

Boone left the party on a Saturday in February to go hunting for buffalo. He traveled about a day away, killed a buffalo, put it on his packhorse and was headed back to the camp when he discovered a group of Indians in hot pursuit.

The weather was cold and snowing and he tried to pull the meat off his horse to make a getaway, but because of the cold he could not loosen the straps he fashioned with buffalo hide. He tried to pull out his knife, intending to cut the straps away. But his knife was sheathed with blood on it and the blood congealed and froze the blade into its sheath. His hands were too greasy to pull it out.

Boone looking at the Indians closing in on him began to run. The Indians gave chase. Across the river and through the woods, Boone ran and still the Indians remained close and closing in. Suddenly shots rang out. The powder horn around Boone's shoulder cut loose from his body. Bullets peppered his feet. He ran until he could run no more, put his rifle against a tree and waited for the Indians. They surrounded him. He surrendered.

The Shawnee warriors took him to a larger party of Indians led by several Frenchmen. Among the Indian leaders were Black Fish, Captain Will and a black interpreter, Pompey.

Boone recognized Captain Will as an Indian who had captured him in 1769. He walked up to him and greeted him. Soon other Indians came around to shake his hand and greet him, as if he were an old friend.

Black Fish asked Boone about the men at the salt lick and told him he was going to kill them. Boone knew his men were unprepared for any attack because it was winter and they weren't expecting any Indians in the area. The attack would come on a Sunday when they would likely be dispersed and lounging around.

Boone told Blackfish that if he promised not to mistreat the men or run them through the Indian "gauntlet" he would ask the men to surrender. Black Fish agreed.

4

Boone and the Indians traveled to the river camp. Boone walked out on the opposite bank, shouted to the men and told them the situation. They agreed to surrender. The Indians appeared and took them prisoner.

They set out for Chillicothe, Ohio, the site of the Indian camp. Before they arrived at the settlement, Black Fish told Boone he had to run the gauntlet. Boone reminded him that he had promised that his men would not have to run the gauntlet. Black Fish said the agreement did not include their leader – the one who made the agreement.

Boone chose to get the ordeal over with before they arrived at the Indian village. Braves cleared the snow and made a space for themselves to stand across from each other. They held tomahawks, clubs, branches and other articles to swing at Boone. He charged through their human tunnel. Boone ran in a zigzag manner and managed to avoid most of the blows and knocked over an Indian in the process.

He was only slightly hurt.

Black Fish seemed to conclude Boone was worthy of being his son. Eventually, the party arrived at Chillicothe and then a group of Indians on March 10, 1778, with French leaders took Boone to Detroit. Boone tells of it in his autobiography.

"I and 10 of my men were conducted by 40 Indians to Detroit where we arrived on the 30th day and were treated by Gov. Hamilton, the British commandant at that post, with great humanity."

Such is Boone's view of the notorious "Hair Buyer."

During the war many prisoners were brought to Detroit by Indians and the area often included Kentucky homesteaders, black slaves and other victims. Hamilton made the village a center of Indian activity and he was constantly asking his government for more money to use to supply Indians with blankets, trinkets and goods to keep them working for the British side.

Boone's youngest son, Nathan, told a historian in the 1820s about his famous father's stay at Detroit.

5

When the Indian party arrived and Hamilton learned Boone was among them and that he was the officer in charge of the party, he invited him to his quarters for the evening. He fed him and asked him about any information regarding British forces and American movements.

Boone told him the Kentuckians had heard of the capture of British General John Burgoyne with some 6,000 troops by American General Horatio Gates near Albany, New York. The surrender occurred in October 1777. Hamilton asked Boone not to tell the Indians. Boone told him he already had.

Boone also said that because of Indian raids, the settlers had not been able to plant crops and that by June there would be no food in Kentucky and no relief was expected from the new government.

Hamilton apparently saw an opportunity to bring the settlers to his side. He offered Black Fish 100 British pounds to ransom Boone. But Black Fish refused. His intention was to make Boone his son.

Boone drew sympathy from other settlers in the city.

"Several English gentleman there, being sensible of my adverse fortune, and touched with human sympathy, generously offered a friendly supply for my wants, which I refused, with many thanks for their kindness; adding, that I never expected it would be in my power to recompense such unmerited generosity," Boone wrote in his autobiography.

Hamilton ordered the king's commissary to supply him a horse, saddle, bridle and blanket and a quantity of silver trinkets to use as currency.

The horse he was given turned out to be a pony.

On April 10, Boone's fellow prisoners were left in Detroit while Black Fish took him back to Chillicothe and his camp to be adopted into the tribe.

Boone went along with the adoption, had his hair pulled out and went through all the physical endurance tests to enter the tribe. During that time he secretly looked for an opportunity to escape. He played along with his role as adopted son, hoeing corn, letting Indians win rifle-shooting contests and showing Indians at various times that he had no intention of running away. He also learned of plans for an Indian attack on Boonesborough.

One day the Indians went turkey hunting. All the braves scattered in pursuit of the prey and Boone saw his chance. He scattered their horses and despite the protests of some Indian women, he saddled his pony and took off.

The Indians pursued Boone after they returned to camp but decided their escapee would get lost and eventually come back. Instead, Boone rode all night and into the next morning on a straight course for his settlement. That morning he stopped to rest his pony. Its legs were lame from the ride, so he unsaddled it, put the saddle and bridle in a tree and took the blanket and his rifle and small provisions of powder and shot he had carefully saved among the Indians and set out on foot.

Before nightfall he arrived at the Ohio River across from what is now Maysville, Kentucky. There he took two dried logs and tied them together with grapevine, took off his clothes and put them on his raft along with his rifle and powder and pushed the raft ahead of him across the river.

On the other side, cold and exhausted he found a place under some trees to spend the night. He pulled his horse blanket around him and slept. The next day his feet were hurting him so he peeled bark from an oak tree, ground it up and made a poultice that he put on his feet. It helped.

The last day after passing the Blue Licks where he was captured, he killed a buffalo, then cooked and ate his first hot and delicious meal in many days. He cut out the tongue of the beast to give to his young son, Daniel, whom he expected to find waiting for him at Boonesborough.

When he arrived at the settlement – a 160-mile journey in three days – he found the fort unprepared for the Indian attack. He also

7

found his family had left and gone back to North Carolina, thinking he was dead. Only his daughter, Jemima, who had married a young settler, remained at the fort along with other families.

Boone set about strengthening defenses for the fort. And then led a raid back across the Ohio River against an Indian village to both intimidate the Indians and gain intelligence about their raiding party.

On August 8, a group of more than 400 Indians, and 40 Frenchmen arrived outside Boonesborough and demanded the settlement's surrender. Among the Indians was Boone's adopted "father" Black Fish. Boone and two others went out to talk to Black Fish and the other officials. Black Fish had letters from Hamilton in Detroit advising Boone to surrender the fort.

Hamilton wrote Boone that if he surrendered, everyone was guaranteed a safe passage to Detroit and if they lost property because of the surrender, the British government would reimburse them. Anyone holding office in the American cause would be given the same rank with the British.

Boone asked for time to talk to the others. He already knew his answer.

Two days later he said, "No."

Black Fish was surprised at Boone's answer. He proposed a treaty with representatives from the settlement. Boone suspected trickery and so chose eight others, including his brother Squire to meet the Indians outside the fort for the treaty.

Boone also stationed sharpshooters ready to fire should trouble break out. As the treaty concluded two Indians per each white man grabbed their arms to "shake hands." Black Fish grabbed Boone who understood "capture" was on Black Fish's mind. He threw Black Fish to the ground, the other Indian let go and Boone charged into a third Indian who had raised the peace pipe/tomahawk to swing at Boone. The glancing blow cut into the back of Boone's neck and shoulder.

Shots rang out from both sides and the men ran back into the fort. Squire Boone and Daniel were injured.

8

For nine days they endured a siege of the fort. The Indian attackers tried flaming arrows and digging a tunnel and frontal assaults but the little group inside proved their match. When the settlers became aware of the tunnel scheme, they dug their own tunnel at an angle in front of the Indians so their tunnel would collapse.

One settler inside the fort, David Bundrin was shot in the forehead. Settlers later described how he sat unspeaking for three days wiping brain tissue from his wound. He rocked his body back and forth and on the third day, died – his brain apparently drained outside of his body.

Jemima, Boone's daughter, was hit with a spent ball from a rifle in the back. Her wound was not serious.

Black Fish was shot in the battle and would later die of his wounds. Pompey, the black translator for the French and Indians also died in the battle. One story has it that he climbed a tree and was acting as a sniper against the fort until Boone shot him out of the tree. Boone's son, Nathan, discounted the story.

The win became a key victory for the cause of the American settlers.

As for Hamilton, bad decisions regarding frontier justice caught up with him and he was indicted by the British government for hanging two men. He left Detroit to what is now Indiana. While there, American Col. George Rogers Clark heard about his presence and early one morning captured him. He was later taken to Virginia and tried.

The paradox of Detroit during the war involved its center as an Indian raider headquarters and also as a place of safety for a group of Protestant Moravian missionaries and their Deleware Indian converts.

The new military commandant of Detroit Major Arent Schuyler De Peyster ordered the Moravians to Detroit, because he was worried about them acting as spies for the Americans.

In actuality, the Moravians took no sides and just preached the gospel of Jesus Christ successfully to the Deleware Indians.

Those implementing De Peyser's order also ordered the Christian Deleware Indians to be rounded up as well as the Moravians and sent to Sandusky.

In early 1782 missionaries and their Indians were preparing for the move. As a group of Delewares packed to make their way to Sandusky from the village of Gnadenhutten they were taken prisoner by a group of Americans from Virginia and told to prepare to die. That night, as the Indians prayed with bowed heads one American assailant after another crushed their skulls with a hammer. In all 90 Indians, including men, women and children were killed.

The British were horrified and the Indians enraged. The Moravian missionaries were brought to Detroit with surviving Christian Indians and they were granted permission from the Chippewa Indians to create a village above the present site of Mount Clemens. There they built houses, planted gardens and crops and labored until 1786 and the close of the war. They were allowed to sell the improved land. Some members of the settlement moved back to Ohio and others went on to Canada to create another village.

As for Daniel Boone, he survived the war and made no more treks into the Michigan region. His later years would be spent in what is now West Virginia and then Missouri and beyond. But Michigan can boast association with the famous frontiersman and pioneer who spent 10 days in Detroit.

Chapter 2:
HISTORIAN OVERBOARD!

Clarence Monroe Burton's name is familiar to history buffs and citizens in the Detroit area for his historical collection donated to the Detroit Public Library. The University of Michigan graduate joined a title and abstract company in the 1870s that eventually became the successful Burton Abstract and Title Co.

Burton died in 1932.

Burton's hobby was history. He wrote and published papers on Detroit's history that became the book "When Detroit Was Young" published in 1951 for the city's 250th birthday. During his lifetime he was president of the Michigan Pioneer and Historical Society and a member of the Michigan

11

Historical Commission. He was founder and president of the Detroit Historical Society.

Burton collected a wide variety of historical material that later became part of the Detroit Public Library and is available to researchers today. But Burton could have done none of this had he not been fished out of the Pacific Ocean as an infant in his mother's arms.

How did he get there?

It's an interesting story.

Dr. Charles S. Burton arrived in Michigan from New York in 1849 and tried to establish a medical practice in what was then the small village of Battle Creek.

However, the young physician's apparent financial struggles caused him to become a sometime journalist in the town. And then gold fever arrived.

With his wife Ann Eliza Burton and a young son, he joined a wagon train in 1853 headed for California. The end of their journey was a mining camp on the Feather River in Northern California in the rugged Sierra Nevada Mountains. The mining community took the name Whiskey Diggings. Gold was first discovered in the region in 1850 and soon gold mining towns such as Whiskey Diggings, Rabbit Creek, Howland Flat and Poker Flat sprung up as mostly men from the East came to find their fortunes.

With two partners, the young doctor mined gold by sifting the dirt, looking for nuggets hidden in the soil and rock. There was actually gold to be found. Whiskey Diggings contained a rich deposit. He also continued his profession, attending to the health needs of the mining community.

Life would have been very difficult for his wife. Few women of any good reputation were in the camps and the atmosphere of the wild-and-wooly West was not the best for a young family. One day in mid-November 1853 the doctor was called across the mountain to help a patient. Before he could return, a snowstorm blocked the roads. Snowstorms in the Sierra Nevadas can be terrible. During a winter in those years, 15 feet of snow was not unusual and the snow didn't leave until June.

Birth pangs began in his young wife.

With the young doctor stranded and only one of her husband's partners attending, Ann Burton gave birth to her second son, Clarence Monroe Burton on Nov. 18. The couple and young family wintered in California and by September 1854 decided to return to Michigan with the gold they'd been able to mine. It is very possible they didn't want to spend another winter in the mountains with a bunch of rowdy men and the responsibility of two young boys.

They purchased tickets on a new steamer, the Yankee Blade, owned by Cornelius Vanderbilt's company.

The 274-foot paddle-wheeler churned out of San Francisco Bay and headed south along the coast.

The goal was to make the passage to Panama and then the family would travel across the strait and get another ship for the East Coast.

The captain of the ship, Henry Randall, chose a course next to the coast despite the fog. Rumors abounded that the ship was in a race with another steamer to make it first to Panama and that the company would pay the captain a bonus if he beat the competitor.

13

On the ship were about 900 other passengers, many of them returning to the East Coast with gold in their pockets or in their baggage. Inside the ship's safe, carried in the stern of the boat was $153,000 in gold nuggets.

The ship traveled down the coast and by the next day continued its course near the coast despite heavy fog and near-zero visibility. Passengers later reported there was no slackening in the speed of the ship. During the afternoon, the confident captain went into the bar to have a drink with a passenger. They sat down just as the ship plowed into the rocks near Point Concepcion and about a mile offshore.

The ship began to sink and the captain ordered the lifeboats overboard. As women and children were boarding, he also got into a boat and left his teenage son in charge. He said he wanted to find a landing place for the passengers.

Meanwhile, a gang of thugs, led by a Jim Turner who already was in trouble with the law in San Francisco, emerged from below deck. They began to rob passengers of jewelry and gold.

Mrs. Burton had sewn in her skirt a large gold nugget. Dr. Burton had purchased his partners' shares of the nugget because it couldn't be divided. During the confusion of the grounding and rush for lifeboats, she became separated from her husband and oldest child. While holding onto Clarence she tried to step into a lifeboat and fell into the water, the weight of the gold nugget weighed her down.

Men in the lifeboat immediately reached out and plucked them out of the sea. Mother and son – and nugget – made it ashore and somehow rejoined Dr. Burton and the oldest son.

More than 30 passengers drowned when another lifeboat overturned near the shore and some passengers drowned trying to swim to shore from the broken boat as darkness approached.

A passenger of the ship, A. T. Harrison drew a sketch of the wreck that later became a lithograph that is contained in the introduction of the book: "When Detroit Was Young."

Many of the ship's survivors spent 10 days on the shore before being rescued by another boat and returned to San Francisco where another passage could be booked. It's not known how the family returned to New York. But when they did, they still possessed the nugget of gold and sold it for $825.

As for the ship's gold, divers led by the captain tried to salvage some of it in the months that followed and eventually much of the gold in the hold was recovered. Officials arrested Samuel Kenny for some of the robberies aboard the ship but the ringleader, Turner, was not caught.

In the summer of 1855 the Burton family returned to Michigan. Dr. Burton started a practice in Hastings, where then-toddler Clarence grew up. He went to the University of Michigan when just 16 and graduated in 1874 from law school.

While at the university he apparently decided to make the study of local history a hobby. As he began his career at the abstract and title office, he started collecting books and documents related to the history of Detroit, the history of Michigan and other places. He would become a leading force in preserving state history and the history of Detroit.

He survived becoming "history" to preserve it.

CHAPTER 3:
WINDS OF PROMISE

Crowds of onlookers from the city known in modern times more for breweries than balloons craned their necks below him. Their eyes fastened upward as he continued to ascend into the almost cloudless blue sky.

"Professor Steiner" looked down at the hundreds of faces. We don't know his first name or whether he was true "professor" or not. But he definitely knew enough about the art of ballooning to attempt and succeed in crossing Lake Michigan after a launch from Milwaukee, Wisconsin.

As the professor stood in his gondola, his hot air balloon christened "The City of Milwaukee" stretched out above him. It was July 4, 1871, and the city had become the center of celebration and remembrance of America's Independence Day for hundreds of city residents and area visitors.

As the nation celebrated 95 years of freedom, Wisconsin was enjoying 23 years as a state in the union. Its rich forests, mines, lakeshore, farmland and opportunities attracted lots of new immigrants all in the mood to honor their new land. It was a day for horse racing, dressing up, parades and lemonade along with other beverages. As part of the celebration Steiner took his balloon to a park near the lakeshore and fired it up. A bright sun, blue skies and gentle breeze meant this was an ideal day to attempt to cross the Big Lake into Michigan. As far as he knew, it had never been done before.

He was confident of his chances being a veteran aeronaut.

At 5:15 p.m. with the balloon filled with air and friends and a crowd of onlookers, he lifted off. Inside the gondola were eight bags of sand to provide 400 pounds of ballast, an anchor with 100 feet of rope, a barometer to tell him what height he was traveling and a thermometer and overcoat.

The ballast determined how quickly he would rise and the anchor and rope would be needed for landing. He was literally a ship afloat in the air and to land he would likely need to tie himself to some object to get down safely.

The balloon floated up and away at a 45-degree angle from its launching pad as friends yelled encouragement. He gained an altitude of 5,000 feet and kept floating on a northeasterly course until 6:30 p.m. Steiner believed he was making good time. The warm summer air below became slightly chilly as he gained altitude. He estimated he was 50 miles from Milwaukee and a short distance past the halfway mark of the Big Lake.

Amazingly, the city remained in view as well as the small lakes around it. He could make out the smoky haze surrounding the rolling mill. Waukesha and Racine could be seen. Lake Michigan proved breathtaking. Lots of vessels cut through the water. Some were under sail and others under steam power. He counted as many as he could see – 46 vessels. Some appeared headed for Chicago, others for Milwaukee, and others possibly to Grand Haven or Holland and others north toward the straits to Mackinac Island and Lake Huron.

As time passed, the Wisconsin shore grew more distant and he climbed to 10,000 feet in hopes of a better wind current to take him across the water. The beautiful view of the lake now offered the opportunity to see both shores. At 10,000 feet it seemed as though the balloon just floated in place. The sun began sinking in the west.

Steiner drank in the colors and sights that to his knowledge no one before him had ever had the opportunity to experience.

"I felt as if I were monarch of all I surveyed and no one could dispute my right," he later told a Milwaukee Sentinel reporter. However, at that altitude and station above the lake, it became very quiet. That bothered the aeronaut. "Oh solitude, where are thy charms."

Looking beneath the gondola he spotted three ships. The relative positions of the balloon and the ships did not change. It was time to try and find a current of air to carry him into Michigan or he would have to stay over the lake all night. He tossed some sand overboard and increased his altitude to 12,000 feet according to the barometer. Now the current seemed to carry him northward but parallel to the shore.

Steiner decided he would descend through 10,000 feet and try and find another current more apt to take him on an easterly direction and into the more populated areas of the state. He pulled on the cord that let the hot air escape from the bag above him. The balloon began to make its descent. At around 5,000 feet he found a current that would carry him along at 35 mph to 40 mph toward the Michigan shore in a southeasterly direction toward Saint Joseph. At that point the balloon was near the center of the lake and on a line drawn from Milwaukee to Grand Haven.

The sun disappeared and the stars began to come out in the sky above him. There seemed to be a huge fireball rising in the east! No, wait, it was just the moon. The moonlight provided lots of light as he reached the Michigan shore. He floated above the great forest of pine, oak, and ash and started to look for a place to throw out his anchor.

"Boom!" A cannon fired in the distance. Someone was celebrating the Fourth. He had crossed the lake and in his zigzag pattern estimated he covered about 150 miles. The wind kept carrying him above the forests and he could not discern any good place to land. Without the sun, the air became very cool. The thermometer with him showed it was 34 degrees. Over the lake, the temperature never dropped below 40 degrees despite his high altitude.

At 10 p.m., he could discern clouds and a storm moving in from the southwest and the direction of Chicago. It was time to land. Steiner prepared his anchor and checked the rope so it would uncoil properly as he tossed it over the side. He adjusted his bags of ballast to ensure they wouldn't fall out in the sudden jerk of the anchor taking hold of something below.

As he pulled on the cord to let out gas, farmhouses and other roads became discernible. He heard someone speaking on the road. Then, plainly, he could hear the sounds of men and women and a wagon with its wooden wheels making its way down the road.

"Hello down there," he yelled. No answer. "Hellooooo."

The women and men looked up.

"Who speaks!" a young man shouted. Then he saw dark mass of the balloon above. "What is that?"

Steiner told them he was going to throw out his anchor. Would they help him with his balloon?

"Balloon? Certainly."

The anchor dropped from the gondola. It caught in a rail fence and tore down several lengths of rail. Finally it caught in a small shrub and held. Steiner started pulling the rope in and the balloon to the earth.

The men and women in the wagon stopped a short distance away, astonished.

"Where did you come from?"

"Milwaukee," he replied.

The City of Milwaukee collapsed after Steiner shut down the heater. The men and women were dressed in their best clothes – this was a holiday and they were headed for an Independence Day dance. Steiner asked the men their names. "Albert H. Cornell and W. Clounce" came the replies.

Despite their nice attire, they helped Steiner wade through the field of clover and pack up his balloon. Soon the balloon, gondola and heating components were all packed onto the wagon. The couples with the professor hitching a ride, continued their drive into Mattawan, four miles northwest from where the balloon landed.

Both taverns in the village were full of celebrants who had arrived to dance. Steiner sat up all night and shared about his

21

experience with people in the tavern. The next morning he loaded the balloon on a train to take him the 12 miles into Kalamazoo where he switched to a train bound for Grand Haven.

At Grand Haven he purchased a ticket and shipped across the lake on the "Ironsides" and arrived back in Milwaukee with his balloon at 7 a.m. on July 6th.

The good professor soared into history and had his flight recorded by the Milwaukee Sentinel, New York Times and possibly many other newspapers around the country that reprinted the Milwaukee Sentinel article. One Michigan newspaper was the Big Rapids Independent.

The good professor's journey over the forests of Michigan certainly proved to be good timing on his part. Just more than two months later, the city of Holland and Saugatuck and much of the Allegan County forest he cruised above would be charcoal. Much of the state would be in flames. Indeed, much of his own state would be in flames.

But that is another story.

Chapter Four:
"Fiery Fiend" of 1871

While the nation's South continued to struggle under reconstruction policies of the Republican administration in Washington D.C. in 1871 and the Ku Klux Klan made headlines from South Carolina, the Northern states were booming with industry and growth.

Pioneers with dreams of greater lands and more bountiful opportunities headed west from Minnesota into the Dakotas and beyond.

Native Americans struggled against the loss of their hunting lands and way of life.

In Michigan, the rush for timber shifted into full gear. Cities, villages and lumber camps were springing up across the north as timber scouts reported the magnificent stands of trees needed to build up the nation's houses and booming commercial areas.

Railroad grades and the iron highways that followed still were being surveyed and laid across the northern Lower Peninsula.

Lumber speculators were getting rich. Timber rights could be purchased for $1.50 an acre and the stands of virgin oak, maple, white pine, hemlock, beech and other trees were beyond belief.

Immigrants from England, Sweden, Norway, Germany, Poland continued to land in New York, searching for better lives and opportunities in the growing nation. Many chose Michigan as their final destination, lured by the promise of the forests, the farmland and the lakes and rivers.

As crews cut into the state's forest stands with their axes and saws, and sawmills sprang up beside rivers and streams, the forest floor in many areas became choked with the byproducts of the timber industry.

Settlers cut trees to clear farmland for their wheat, corn and hay and the forests became littered with more brush and half-burnt logs and trees.

Weather during the summer failed to cooperate. A nation-wide drought dried out the forests and fields and prepared the path for great tragedy across the northern states.

The rains of September failed to materialize to prepare the wheat for harvest. The forests were dry and so were the fields. Some harvested stacks of straw and hay dotted the acreage.

Then came the destroying winds from across the lake. Some Michigan residents at the time believed they carried embers from the fires that started in Chicago on Oct. 8. Many little forest fires already were burning in Michigan and the wind fanned the flames. Regardless of how the fires began, what soon became clear was that the Midwest from Minnesota to Wisconsin and Chicago, Michigan and Ontario would suffer from the flames of disaster.

News accounts of the disasters began with the great tragedy that struck Chicago. Soon telegraph operators from Michigan and Wisconsin would be sending reports of a living inferno that turned their communities into the ashes of furnace debris.

The New York Times gave the Chicago fires the prominent spot on the front page for two days and then the news of the Michigan and other fires showed up.

Among others, the cities of Holland, Saugatuck and Manistee on the state's western shore became smoke and rubble.

In Holland, the Dutch immigrants already had invested 24 years into prospering their pioneer efforts. Churches, saw mills, blacksmiths, stores of all sorts were up and operating and starting to thrive. A channel had been dug from Lake Michigan into Black Lake and the community boasted docks for lake freighters and the status of an incorporated city.

On Sunday, the winds arrived and embers from fires burning southwest of the city flew into the city. Those were the sparks of tragedy. Soon most of the city was ablaze and by the time the fires roared through the downtown businesses, houses and into the swamp northwest of the city, more than 300 homes were gone along with 75 businesses, 15 manufacturing firms, four churches and 45 other buildings.

Newspaper accounts speak of people fleeing before the flames for their lives and not being able to save clothing or bedding or anything. The miracle of the fire is that only one life was lost – although initial reports spoke of five people dying in the flames.

Businesses claimed by flames included a tannery, factories that produced staves for barrels, two saw mills, a bank, the post office, a brewery, barber shops, meat markets and saloons and many other stores. Also lost to the fire were the buildings that contained the "Gazetter" – the city's English language newspaper and three Dutch newspapers, the "Groudwet," "Hollander" and "Wachter."

Hope College survived the inferno, as did First Reformed Church. However, Second Reformed, Third Reformed, a Methodist congregation and Episcopal congregation all lost their structures of worship.

A telegraph account from the days of the disaster gives some scope of the tragedy.

"It is reported that all the region of country between Holland and Saugatuck is devastated. Farm houses, barns, crops, everything having been swept away. The people are suffering beyond expression and need assistance."

Barns and stores and crops from Fennville to Nunica fell to flames. St. Joseph was saved by some rain.

Fire arrived in the north and east and south. The majority of the citizens of the Lower Peninsula found themselves in peril.

26

In the north-central region of the state, the Cedar Springs Clipper newspaper reported a block of stores in the village destroyed by fire but a general destruction was stopped by the efforts of citizen fire brigades.

In Newaygo County, several homes, farm buildings and lumber shanties were lost. The citizens of the city of Newaygo somehow managed to keep the flames out of the city.

For a time, Big Rapids was in danger. A Capt. Stewart Ives told the Detroit Post that the city was surrounded and citizens were fighting hard to keep it out. Three homes burned on the outskirts of the city. Howard City, Morley and other villages also were threatened.

In the north, Leelenau County's Glen Haven was completely destroyed by flames. Offshore, a steamship called the Mohawk reported the Manitou Islands were ablaze.

At Manistee, a hub of the great lumbering effort in the northwest part of the state, 4,000 residents spent their Sunday quietly, many worshipping at church. Their faith would be sorely tested in the following 24 hours.

Gen. B. M. Cutcheon, a city resident, gave an account of the day that was published in the Grand Rapids Eagle newspaper. He said the city was divided into four wards along the Manistee River, Lake Michigan and Manistee Lake.

Within the city, a 20-acre parcel of dead hemlock trees stood "as combustible as gunpowder."

On Sunday, Oct. 8, a fire began in the Fourth Ward and burned furiously in a tract of land that had been harvested of trees and had piles of brush and debris. Citizens and the fire department worked most of the day to put out the flames and by sundown thought they had it taken care of. The fire engine returned to the fire barn.

"It was scarcely housed when the wind, which had been blowing highly all day, rose to a perfect gale," Cutcheon reported. "At about 2 o'clock while the fire in the Fourth Ward was raging, an alarm whistle was heard from the east side of Manistee Lake, and through thick smoke it was discovered that the large steam mill of Magill & Canfield, on Blackbird Island, was in flames. In an incredibly short space of time, mill, boarding house, stables, shops, docks and lumber were consumed."

With the darkness, a glow in the southwest revealed the pine forest blazing on the shoreline of Lake Michigan.

"About 9:30 p.m., just as people were returning from evening services, the fire alarm again sounded, and everyone now was on the alert for the wind was blowing a fierce gale," Cutcheon said.

Fire spread to the large steam mill and lumberyard owned by a John Canfield at the mouth of the river. There were tugs waiting for favorable weather to pull out into the lake and a boarding house and many other dwellings. Along the beach, acres were covered with pine sawdust and along the river and piers, several hundred cords of dry pine slabs were piled for as fuel for the tug boats.

Firefighters found themselves immediately overwhelmed.

"The burning sawdust, whirled by the gale in fiery clouds, filled the air. Hundreds of dry, pitchy slabs sent up great columns of red flame that swayed in the air like mighty banners of fire, swept across Manistee and almost instantly, like great fiery tongues, licked up the government lighthouse, built

28

at the cost of nearly $10,000 and situated 150 feet from the north bank of the river."

The mill also was gone and the situation grew worse.

Gale-force winds also swept fore into the south of the town, but not before the flames devoured three farmhouses, all their barns and outbuildings and crops. Then the fire swept into the southern section of town.

A correspondent from the Detroit Tribune takes up the story.

"It now caught in the buildings and continued its resistless march sweeping northward through the place for the width of three blocks," the correspondent reported.

The fire then changed direction and headed down Main Street for four blocks, jumped the river at the Maple Street bridge and destroyed all the property on the north side of the river.

"Many families were driven from their homes without a moments warning. Children were snatched from their beds and carried off by their mothers to seek a place of safety, while the fathers were about attempting to save other houses, not dreaming that their own homes were in danger."

Cutcheon spoke of the terror of the moments.

"The fire now came roaring through the dead hemlocks south of the blocks included between Maple and Oak Streets in the Second Ward. The flames leaped to the summits of the great hemlocks, 70 or 80-feet high, and threw out great flags of fire against the lurid heavens. The scene was grand and terrible beyond description."

Many people ran from flames in one part of the city only to find another part of the town in flames as well. Cutcheon's own family ran across a bridge over the Manistee River and the bridge burned behind them. The smoke and fire on the north side almost destroyed them.

Much of the city center became a sea of fire. Cutcheon said firefighters barely escaped with their lives.

"The steam fire engine burned in the street where it stood, the men and horses barely escaping with their lives. About 3 o'clock (a.m.) the wind abated, but the work of ruin was complete."

In the First Ward three buildings survived, the Catholic Church, the Ward schoolhouse and a small home. In the Second Ward six blocks of homes were gone between Oak and Maple Streets and two-dozen buildings near the river's mouth. The Fourth Ward survived almost intact except for the opulent house owned by the banker.

Monday almost 1,000 people were homeless, including Cutcheon and his family.

"Then was seen a spectacle to gladden the heart," Cutcheon said. "Every house that remained was opened to receive the sufferers. Hearts and hands were as open as the homes. We almost felt it worthwhile to suffer for the sake of witnessing how much of generosity was latent in human nature."

Flames broke out again on Monday night and the remaining portion of town was saved by valiant efforts of the citizens and a rain that fell at midnight.

As Manistee struggled and Holland burned, citizens around much of the rest of state found the same enemy trying to raze their settlements.

Muskegon residents fought flames fanned in the tamarack forests between Grand Haven and their city. Residents dug pits to bury their possessions under dirt if need be. But courageous efforts by citizens saved the city.

At Wayland, almost every able-bodied person fought flames that seemed intent on entering and devouring the village. Citizens saved the city. Grand Rapids mounted a huge firefighting effort with its citizens and kept the flames at bay until some rain arrived, something some residents attributed to divine intervention.

Accounts in the Detroit Post and Saginaw Daily Enterprise reported fires around the Grand Rapids area and south.

"All along the line of the Grand Rapids and Indiana road, both north and south, on the line of the Detroit and Milwaukee, on both sides of the city, south on the line of the Lake Shore, and on the Grand River Valley division, the flames were raging furiously at various points, on both sides of the track. The heat was so intense along some of the roads that glass in the car windows was cracked in passing trains."

An Oct. 9 dateline out of Lansing reported in the Big Rapids Independent newspaper: "The woods are on fire on all sides of the State Agricultural College. All college exercises are suspended and professors and students are engaged day and night in checking the fiery element."

Efforts by the students and citizens saved the college. The students would later be rewarded with a special oyster dinner put on by the president's wife and other ladies of the college. Classes resumed on Oct. 11.

In Saginaw, fires encircled the city, and citizens rallied to save it.

"Business was suspended and while the engines were kept playing in the vicinity of the Sunday night fire, the citizens, organized in six companies of 100 each, in as many subdivisions of the city, were engaged all day yesterday and during the night, in fighting the fiery element, and trying to save their houses and property," the Saginaw Daily Enterprise reported.

A settlement called Dutchtown near Chesaning was wiped out. Swan Creek, Owosso and Hemlock suffered great losses in housing and crops to the flames. At many places, plank roads through swamps burned up.

At Saginaw and East Saginaw flames surrounded the cities. Firefighters held them off.

"All along the Saginaw River we hear of nothing but narrow escapes and destruction of property, but the total damage is much smaller than was expected, considering the terrible fires in the surrounding woods," reported the Saginaw Daily Enterprise.

Midland also was surrounded and escaped only through the efforts of its citizens. Freeland citizens fought flames and the railroad tracks between their village and Midland were covered with burning trees so that rails twisted. At Essexville, Kawkawlin, Wenona, Standish and Bay City flames surrounded the cities. A railroad bridge burned across the Pinconning River.

On the north side of Saginaw Bay, Tawas and Alabaster were threatened by flames.

Human suffering and disaster then seemed to concentrate in the Thumb.

There were 23 townships burned, 18 townships that suffered some tragedy and in the Thumb 90 percent of the housing leveled – most of it along the coast.

Towns such as Forestville and White Rock on the coast were thriving with the timber industry.

"The news from St. Clair and Huron counties of this date is of the most distressing character. All that portion of the state east of Saginaw Bay and north of a point 40 miles above Port Huron has been completely swept by fire. A number of persons perished, and it is feared we have not heard the worst. The flourishing villages of Forestville, White Rock, Elm Creek, Sand Beach and Huron City are completely destroyed. Nothing has yet been heard from Port Austin or Port Crescent, but it is hardly possible that they escaped," reported the New York Times on Oct. 11.

The human suffering, loss of farm animals and crops with the winter season around the corner brought the state to its knees.

The gale arrived in Huron and Tuscola counties about midnight Oct. 8. Slumbering forest fires in the townships of the Thumb sprang to life. Then the sleeping pioneer farmers and villages just became fuel for what many newspapers dubbed the "fiery fiend."

Settlers inland from the lake came tearing into the lakeside villages in buggies and wagons pulled by horses with wild eyes trying to flee the flames. At Sand Beach, now Harbor Beach, everything quickly burned except a boarding house and store and the Rice shingle-mill lying under a hill near the water.

"The inhabitants were driven out and many sought refuge in the lake, throwing the water over themselves to protect their

33

bodies and faces from the intense heat occasioned by the burning of a great number of buildings near the shore. This town is almost totally ruined, its milling interest destroyed and its population scattered far and wide. A number of its people are at Port Huron and other points on the shore and desirous of returning and rebuilding the town," reported the New York Times.

On Sunday night White Rock, located south of what is now Harbor Beach, was entirely destroyed. The village had some 300 inhabitants. An elderly woman burned to death, her body with head and limbs mostly destroyed was discovered on one of the streets following the fire. Flames also destroyed nearby Forestville.

Detroit resident Preston Brady was visiting White Rock when the fire arrived. His account of the disaster revealed the residents tried to fight the fire but quickly determined the flames were not going to be held back.

Many ran to their homes and grabbed whatever valuables they could carry and ran to the nearest field or forest opening away from the houses. Some people ran to the Lake Huron shore and doused themselves in the water. That proved to be the wisest response.

Brady said he ran into the water and the air became so hot that survivors had to repeatedly plunge beneath the waves to remain unscorched. He spent eight hours in the water, much of the time lying on a log as the waves pounded over him.

Looking around him he saw men up to their waists in water, many holding children and women trying to survive the paradox of the cold waves and hot air.

As the fires died down, people left the water for the shore. There they stood on blackened smoking ash and rubble. Food and shelter was non-existent. On Monday afternoon the steamer Huron arrived and loaded as many as it could onto its deck for a trip to Port Huron.

The New York Times reported Oct 12: "It is said there is but one dock left on the shore about Forestville. A steamer which left Port Huron last night for the relief of the sufferers returned this evening with about 40 men, women and children, five of whom are severely burned. The revenue cutter, "Fessenden," which started for Port Austin, picked up a sailboat on the lake containing Isaac Green, principal owner of Forestville, together with his family and eighteen or 20 others who escaped the flames. The telegraph operator at Forestville escaped through the fire back into the country. All the telegraph offices along the shore have been destroyed, but communication will be restored as soon as the damage done to the lines can be repaired."

The "Fessenden" reached Port Huron after its rescue trip with 17 refugees and two charred bodies.

As fire reports came out of the Thumb, the tragedy became clearer. Huron City, New River and Port Hope lost most of their buildings, as did Forest Bay, Center Harbor and Elm Creek.

Cities that escaped included Port Austin, Cato, and Minden in the interior. Tyre a little settlement just five miles from Minden burned in flames.

A Polish settlement named Cracow was destroyed and residents saved their lives by lying in a deep ditch they had dug to drain the swamps.

Rain on October 14 quenched some of the intensity of the fires but more sunshine quickly posed more problems for more communities as the fires sought more fuel.

In the southeast of the state, Ypsilanti lost buildings to the fires and Monroe County lost many houses, barns and fields of corn and stacks of hay and straw. Hundreds of miles of fences were destroyed.

The aftermath of the fires brought indescribable suffering.

A Detroit Post correspondent reported people found 50 bodies in fields and woods inland from Port Austin. "Some lie on their faces suffocated only, in the apparent attempt to crawl under the stifling smoke for a breath of air. Others are crisp and black."

Another correspondent reported that the wife of a Charles McMillan of Parisville, inland from White Rock, was in her bed with a child only a few hours old when she was forced to flee for her life. "The fire drove her from the bed with the babe in her arms, a child in one hand, and two other children following her. Her mother a little way behind her was caught by the flames while passing through the gateway and perished there."

Michigan Gov. Henry P. Baldwin issued a proclamation on Oct. 16, 1871:

"While you have been occupied in the noble work of furnishing relief to the sore afflicted people of the neighboring city of Chicago, large sections of our own state were being devastated by the terrible scourge of fire.

"Several counties have been almost entirely ruined, thriving cities, towns and villages have been reduced to ashes;

mills giving employment and support to hundreds of families, whole townships of valuable timber, dwellings, barns, crops, and property of every description have been totally destroyed. The destruction of both life and property has been appalling; thousands of our citizens have been rendered homeless and are destitute of the absolute necessities of life.

"The calamity which has befallen our people, terrible as it would be at any time, is doubly so at the commencement of the approaching inclement season of the year, and calls most earnestly upon every citizen of the State, who has escaped the sad disaster, to contribute to promptly and literally toward the relief of these our suffering fellow citizens.

"While contributions for the afflicted people of Michigan have been, and probably will continue to be, made from other states, such cannot be depended upon. Reliance must be placed mainly upon people of our own Commonwealth.

"I therefore appeal to the people of Michigan to meet this emergency with a degree of promptness and liberality measured only by the urgent necessities of the case."

The governor appointed two relief committees, one in Grand Rapids and the other in Detroit. He asked for money, clothing, food and bedding to be forwarded as quickly as possible to the committees.

"Let us remember that it is more blessed to give than to receive."

The burgeoning timber industry took a direct hit. Careless practices by lumberjacks and timber camps didn't help their cause. Many trees and branches would just be left on the forest floor. Stumps and brush would not be cleared out, providing fast fuel for the "fiery fiend" or the more apocalyptic

"Angel of Destruction," as the Big Rapids Independent named it.

Timber camps were burned on the Pine River, three on Sturgeon Creek, many on the Cass River. In Albee, near Chesaning, a mill and all its buildings along with 6,000 to 8,000 feet of lumber was destroyed. A Dr. David Ward of Pontiac lost $100,000 to $200,000 in pine trees.

Assistance flowed into the state from New York City and from many other sources.

Gen. E.M. Lee who commanded the Michigan Cavalry Brigade and later served as governor of the Wyoming Territory arrived in the state and offered stories of the Civil War and other adventures in 12 different lectures. Money from the lectures went to benefit the sufferers in the state.

The citizens of Spring Lake raised at least $1 for each citizen of Holland who suffered. Kalamazoo County commissioners canceled their $2,411 claim against the City of Manistee. The Ottawa County Board of Supervisors ordered Holland city's proportion of county and state taxes spread upon the rolls of other towns.

The Second Reformed Church of Grand Rapids donated $160 to the Michigan Relief Fund after a collection on Sunday, Oct. 22.

Citizens of Detroit, Lansing and Pontiac sent rail cars of relief to Grand Haven to be put onto a ship for Manistee. Flour, clothing and other provisions resulted after pleas from Gen. Cutcheon, who asked for clothing for many of the women of the city who fled the fire in their nightclothes. He also asked for carpenter's tools because all the tools were burnt in the fire.

38

The irony of which cities suffered and which ones were spared was not lost to the editor of the Big Rapids Independent. He wrote:

"Our own city yet stands among the fortunate, but no one can tell how soon it may fall a victim to the march of the resistless conqueror ... The duties of the hour are manifest. Every one should use utmost caution in the use of that element which is so useful a servant to man when under his control, but so terrible a master when unrestrained.

"Everyone should stand ready to be measured by the golden rule. Let every hand be ready to render aid, while the heart acknowledges God's care and kindness in our preservation thus far."

Accounts say more than 200 people across the Lower Peninsula lost their lives in the 1871 blazes and some 2.5 million acres burned. Many more victims could have been lost due to the nature of the pioneering effort and isolation of many in the woods. Millions of dollars were lost and hundreds of tragic stories became to attached to that generation.

The resilience of the Michigan pioneers showed up in how quickly cities such as Holland, Manistee, White Rock and Forestville bounced back.

For many residents in the Thumb the destruction of 1871 was a precursor to a "fiery fiend" that would visit one decade later. The consequences then would be just as bad or worse. Their ability to cope with loss would be sorely tried again.

Chapter Five:
Thumb in '81:
Ashes to Ashes

A new decade in the state ushered in new prosperity and resurrected hopes and dreams for many.

The fire of 1871 seemed relegated to history. The timber industry flourished with the help of railroads that cut into the north woods and allowed previously inaccessible forest stands to be harvested.

Immigrants continued to arrive in the state with dreams of creating new lives for themselves in the forests and farms of the Lower Peninsula and the rich copper and iron ore mines of the Upper Peninsula. Veterans of the Grand Army of the Republic who fought for the Union in the Civil War sought homesteads in the state.

As September approached in 1881, the nation's hearts and minds focused on Long Branch, New Jersey, where beloved

41

President James Abram Garfield lay in his bed with a gunshot wound that would soon claim his life.

In New York City, the talk of the town centered around the financial and corruption scandal at Tammany Hall, the seat of city government. The New York Times published a series of front-page stories exposing the how the city misspent the money entrusted to it.

In the West, the U.S. Army kept busy pursuing Apache Indians who were determined not to waste away on a reservation while miners and ranchers staked claims to the territory they hunted, wandered and lived on for generations.

In Missouri the notorious Jesse James and his gang astounded the nation with a daring train robbery outside Independence, Mo.

As a whole, the Midwest was experiencing another summer of heat and drought. Michigan's forests and fields were extremely dry. Marshes around Saginaw and Bay City lacked moisture and provided potential for disaster. Partially cleared tracts of land with lumber and brush remained throughout the Thumb as settlers tried to wrestle the land from the forest and loggers took what trees they could for the sawmills.

During a normal summer, there would be occasional forest fires and city blazes to deal with. The infrastructure of the state was wood. But none of the fires approached the scale of October 1871 – until September of 1881.

On Sept. 5, residents in the central counties and then the Thumb woke to gale force winds. With the winds arrived the smell of smoke, the sight of flames and then for many the terror of total destruction.

From the Saginaw area through the Thumb telegraph lines connecting communities melted in the heat, cutting communication. Choking clouds of smoke removed the light of day and the flames racing through the tinder-dry forests outran settlers trying to escape them.

Newspapers reported flames in Freeland, around Saginaw, south to Lapeer County. Reports came in of flames advancing throughout the Thumb.

The telegraph operator in Port Sanilac sat at the key on Sept. 6 as the smoke brought darkness and the accounts of the terror swept into town with the smoky ruins of farmers and travelers warning the community of a coming holocaust.

His fingers quickly tapped out these lines: "The whole country is burning up … Fear reigns supreme in all hearts, many people not going to bed."

For Michigan's pioneers, the days of toil in the woods and on the land promised a better future. But on the day the flames and smoke arrived more than one pioneer had the words of the "good book," the Bible, flash through their mind: "The day of the Lord cometh, for it is nigh at hand, A day of darkness and of gloominess, a day of clouds and of thick darkness, … A fire devoureth before them; and behind them flame burneth: the land is as the Garden of Eden before them, and behind them a desolate wilderness; yea, and nothing shall escape them."

More than 200 of them did not escape, swept into eternity by a wall of fire that discriminated against nothing. The heat, smoke and flames became the event which a generation of Thumb residents measured time.

"Was that before the fire, or after the fire?"

Those who heard the question understood what fire was being inferred. The Great Fire of 1881 changed the landscape and the destiny of many settlers. Only a few in modern generations know of their suffering.

Consider those days, the names, the villages and cities – and know the terrible sacrifice made by those who have gone before us. Understand as well, that with every disaster and tragedy, another day shines brighter if only the following generations will learn the lessons of the past.

The locomotive engineer put a scarf across this mouth and tried to see what lay on the tracks ahead. Smoke stung his eyes and he glanced ahead of his locomotive. His small train churned out of St. Louis on the daily run east to Saginaw. As he approached St. Charles, forest on each side of the track seemed to be afire. He pushed forward on the throttle.

Small forest fires had been putting smoke into the air all summer. But as he looked ahead on this day, walls of flame appeared to merge above his tracks. Smoke and flames jumped out as if to challenge him and the train. He determined that he wouldn't give the flames enough time to settle into the oak exteriors of his train cars.

The train passed through the tunnel of fire. Heat hit the cab as if a blast oven doors were opened. The engineer yelled to the fireman to keep an eye on the cars behind. He did not want the train to become a literal fireball. On each side, the roar of the flames could be heard as he passed through a stand of forest only partially logged over. Now the dead branches and trunks on the ground combined with the trees left standing fueled a wind of fire that he had never witnessed before.

44

Miraculously, the cars came through the inferno. As he neared Saginaw and then East Saginaw, smoke hung over the cities and other fires surely must be burning to the south. It was hard not to cough. People could be seen walking with kerchiefs over their noses. He turned to his cab partner.

"You ever read the Bible, Judd?"

"Naw, just the old lady," replied the fireman.

"Well, it's hard to know if hell can be much worse."

"You're telling me, Bill! I ain't going back out there and risking becoming a piece of broiled meat until this thing passes."

Once at the depot the engineer headed toward the telegraph office. He wanted to warn the stations back down the line. Inside, a young man soaked with sweat and pencil in hand was taking down a message. Beside him stood a local newsman. The reporter shook his head as he looked over the telegrapher's shoulder.

"Apocalypse. That's what this is. Apocalypse," he spoke.

On the pad, page after page were reports of countryside burning up.

"Have you tried to get Port Austin?" the newsman asked.

The telegraph operator tapped the station for the city at the tip of the Thumb. No response.

"The lines must be down or burned." The young telegrapher spoke matter-of-factly. He was trying to sound professional but inside his chest his heart beat wildly. The calendar in front of him showed Sept. 5, 1881. But to his mind, it could have been the judgment day. He had heard about the fire that swept the state 10 years earlier and the destruction it had caused.

Now they were living it again. Why? Was God angry?

45

The last reports spoke of Bad Axe, Forestville and other cities in danger.

Temperatures hovered above 90 degrees. The heat was stifling and the promise of rain non-existent – just as it had been for almost two months. Now winds were blowing and fires growing and everything seemed headed to destruction.

In Saginaw, citizens formed battalions of fire brigades and were at work across the city trying to save businesses and homes from the flames leaping outside the city in the forests. But the winds just picked up firebrands from the forest and carried them aloft to porch or home roofs and then the race was underway to extinguish the ember before flames erupted.

The young telegrapher put his mind back to his task. A man ran in with a message about the disaster to be sent to Detroit.

The man reported that two men had just come into the city from Buena Vista Township, a forested area of mostly Indians and a few German families. Their settlement was burning and they narrowly escaped with their lives.

His message also spoke of a man named Christopher Wartenberg, a farmer on the town line road between Saginaw and Kochville, whose house and barn burned. His neighbor across lost a barn. Another man in the same vicinity had his house and barn burned and Albert Ringer, who lived near the Mackinaw Road lost a house and barn.

More trouble was reported northwest and then east of Saginaw.

The engineer's report along with other information filtering in revealed problems west of the city. News from Vassar, to the east, also revealed flames threatening that city. The operator had tried to raise the city, but the wire remained silent. The lines going in must have burned.

Some 65 miles northeast of Saginaw, residents of Bad Axe awoke that day to smoky sunshine. The previous day, Sunday, Septimus Irwin, landlord of the Irwin House Hotel, led a group of men to go out and fight a growing forest fire 10 miles west of Bad Axe. They found the fire in a 12-acre tract of land being cleared. Dry logs had been laid in piles and set afire. The fire spread to other undergrowth nearby and was out of control. The men returned to town and put water barrels in strategic places around the downtown should the fire try and sweep into the city. But later in the day the fire seemed to blow he other way and not much was thought about it.

As residents went about their business on Monday, about 10:30 a.m. the wind picked up and smoke darkened the sky. Winnie Chipman, daughter of the county's prosecuting attorney, noticed the fear in her mother. Mrs. Chipman nervously gathered a few important belongings and told her daughters to follow her to the courthouse.

They stopped at her father's office. Winnie gathered his law books to take to the courthouse and put into the vault of the Register of Deeds. It was the only major building in the city not made of wood. It had been built of mostly brick and boasted a slate roof.

Shortly after lunch, the gale arrived. Wind took fire from the woods and put it into a haystack on the west side of the city. It then took the flaming hay and sent it across the town. Soon the belfry of the Baptist church, a barn and other places received a

flaming piece of the stack. Fire erupted simultaneously in six or
more places.

Women and children ran to the courthouse fighting the
strong wind and trying to get to shelter. Men of the city gathered
and tried to pump water on the fires but the wind gusts proved
too strong. They, too, retreated to the courthouse and tried to stay
alive. As some men pumped water from the courthouse pump
into buckets, others ran to the east side of the building to throw
water on some sanded wooden surfaces.

Fire raged through downtown stores. Chemicals in the drug
store, 36 barrels of kerosene in another store, gunpowder in yet
another caused tremendous explosions and the heat inside the
courthouse became almost unbearable.

Children buried their faces into the dresses of their mothers,
who tried to comfort them knowing that eternity could come at
any moment. Some men were brought into the building after only
a minute outside, their eyes blinded by heat and smoke.

More than a few of the more than 200 people gathered
inside the building were praying.

"We've come to the end of the world, children," one
woman spoke. "Call out on the Lord Jesus."

The courthouse became so hot that paint bubbled on the
walls and leather volumes inside the Register's office started to
crack as all moisture was removed from the air.

As the afternoon wore one, the flames consumed almost
everything possible in the buildings along the Main Street. The
terrible rushing sound of the flames licking up wood and paint
and furniture and memories continued all afternoon. As the
evening came, men searched the city, looking for any caught by

the terrible inferno. Smoke hung heavy everywhere. The ground remained hot.

A survey showed tremendous loss.

The hotel was gone and so were the Baptist and Methodist churches. Home after home was in ashes and rubble. The law office used by the prosecutor and two other attorneys was gone. Winnie was thankful she had saved the books. Amazingly, her home escaped the flames.

Her father arrived that night, braving smoke and flames and walking all the way from Sand Beach carrying a ham and a sack of crackers. He thought people would be hungry.

Thankfully, the fire spared some of the town's store of supplies.

Meanwhile north of the city, two brothers had been building a house for a farmer and decided to return home. The weather turned frightfully dark and smoky.

They climbed into a well.

One of the brothers, Roderick Park, kept thinking about what the older residents had been saying: "The sun is showing the sign of fire, just as in '71."

Fire roared overhead and a wave of heat pushed down inside the well. The brothers stayed there until it seemed as though the flames had past. They climbed out to find total destruction. Park would later share his thoughts

"The earth was scorched and smoldering. Down wind I saw poplars burst into flame. What had been green leaves were so seared by hot winds that they went up with a roar as the fire struck them. … I saw a snake crawling over the hot ground. Instinctively, I moved to kill it, but thought better of that. It had survived the fire. Let it live."

That day the mailman, Ira Humphrey tried to take the mail through the smoking and flaming forests between Marlette and Bad Axe. He never made it. His horse came limping back into Marlette, badly burned. Humphrey's charred body later would be discovered in the black, smoldering woods.

The fire roared toward the Huron Shore, devastating townships and the pioneer settlers trying to put down their roots.

Farmers were caught in fields, their families caught in flight or hidden in wells with scarcely enough water to keep their feet wet.

Michigan newspapers began chronicling the disaster in black and white for all the world to see. Any telegraph wires not yet burned carried news of devastation and loss.

From the Bay City Tribune came the sad story of the Richmond family in Delaware Township. As the fire approached, the family dove into a new 12-foot deep well with about two feet of water in the bottom. When the flames swept past, the top of the well that was covered with boards and planks caught fire. The burning lumber dropped down on the father, mother and five of their six children. All were dead when discovered the next day. The baby, less than a year old, drowned in the water. Fire removed part of the father's head. The oldest boy, 12, was away at a neighbor's and was the only member of the family left alive.

On Sept. 6, The Detroit Evening News told readers that Mrs. Richard Elliott of Five Lakes burned to death in the woods the previous night while she fled fires around her home. In Millington, William Bates' sawmill burned along with lumber, logs and every building around it. A lumberyard belonging to J.C. Smith also fell to flames. Firestorms raced across the entire Thumb.

Accounts recorded that Moore Township was "swept clear." In Flynn Township there was thousands of dollars in damage. In Elk Township buildings, crops and every bridge was destroyed. Excepting the village of Sandusky, "nearly all of Watertown Township was destroyed."

The account speaks of desperate actions by residents to escape the flames.

"A farmer saved his family by taking refuge in a field of buckwheat. A woman in his neighborhood tried to save herself and children by digging a hole and covering the best she could with her hands. They were all subsequently found dead. The little ones had their heads burned to the shoulders."

Initial estimates reported about 500 people lost including 26 bodies found in Moore Township, 60 bodies brought to Sand Beach and an estimated 5,000 people homeless.

A Lexington dateline on Sept. 8, 1881 in the Detroit Free Press carried this account:

"A man driving through Huron County directly toward the spread of fire reported that he met five women entirely naked, each carrying a child. He gave them two flour bags to cover themselves."

Businesses were gone. Farms disappeared.

At the lake on that fateful day, many people dove into the waters and stayed there as the flames burned forest all the way to the shore. The region around Forestville suffered greatly. One man arrived at the shore, almost insane and blind and had to be led into the waters.

Sand Beach was saved from the flames by a change of wind. Inside the city, residents were forced to light lanterns as the air grew darker and smoke descended on the city. Flames would be heard approaching and many ran for the lake. But at the last minute as the roar of fire sounded, the wind switched to the east. The town survived.

Near Forestville on Indian Creek Road a farmer with the good name of Abram Thornton died with his wife, one son and the loss of home, barn and livestock. One son survived.

At Port Hope a wall of fire swept into the village and people ran for the lake. Some residents jumped into wells and died of smoke inhalation. At the lake, people who had driven their wagons and buggies into the water witnessed them burn down to the water line. Many spent the entire night dunking and dousing themselves in the water.

When the sun arose in the morning, one man looked behind him in the water and there sat a bear, unafraid as if domesticated.

County officials and other prominent members of the communities affected issued pleas to the outside world for help.

In a plea to Detroit Free Press readers for aid, a member of the firm of "Corbishley and Doyle" attempted to depict the horrific conditions.

"Our county is burned to a black crisp. Miles and miles of county lay waste and not a green thing to be seen. In whole terms we are burned out and everything is a total loss. Yesterday I helped bury a mother and four children burned to death in the road. This morning brings in reports of 20 more.

"Should there be no general system of relief organized we would be much pleased to have small donations from anyone who might be induced to give in the line of meat, second-hand cook stoves, clothing, etc."

Human suffering and animal suffering mingled. Dead cattle, fried to a crisp, were familiar sights. Some in herds, others alone, lost in the woods or along a creek attempting to flee the flames. In one creek, the water became so hot that the fish boiled. Many bodies of pioneer farmers and families were discovered with their heads and appendages burned off.

Wire accounts of the disaster published in the New York Times moved that city and the New York Stock Exchange to respond.

A front-page story on September 10 began with the headline "Devastated by Flames."

The account goes on to describe high winds that fanned flames cutting off every avenue of escape for some residents.

"One farmer who was plowing with his oxen a few miles from Sand Beach perceived the approaching darkness and started for the house. On reaching home, he found that his wife had gone to a neighbor's house. He then took two his children, his eldest daughter taking three others. Before going many rods they found themselves cut off by the flames. The farmer then turned in another direction and escaped with the two children. His daughter and the other three children were found the next day, all in a heap charred beyond recognition. Up to Wednesday night, 45 bodies have been found within a mile."

Rescue parties found many gruesome sights and heard more tales of narrow escape and tragedy. A Dr. Hoyt reported many people who were badly burned.

"George Ferguson of White Rock, who has been on the road since Monday, reports that he has seen 116 burned bodies; at one place he saw four wagons bearing eight coffins with one

53

man walking behind all alone. It was his family. Another man was following with three coffins."

A dispatch from Port Austin estimated 200 to 300 dead and Bad Axe, Verona, Forest Bay, Richmondville, Charleston, Anderson, Deckerville, Harrisonville and Sandusky all burned. Port Hope, Minden and Ubly suffered partial destruction.

Reports from Saginaw, Tuscola and Lapeer counties also depicted large losses of property.

In Sanilac County, 32 persons were known to be dead. Some 215 families lost homes and farms in Marlette, Flynn, Argyle, Evergreen, Moore, Lamotte and Elmer. A rain fell to help quench the fires, saving other lives and property.

As would-be rescuers traveled through the burned district, they found many settlers sitting in the ashes of their burned houses. Many suffered from burns and other injuries. Many were mentally ill, "bereft of their senses."

A newspaper correspondent sent a report to Chicago of all the devastation. And the move to raise money and aid began in earnest there.

"Whole families in the burned district have been left entirely naked. A correspondent saw people on the road from Port Austin to Cass City digging potatoes and eating corn that had been roasted by the fires; it was all they had left. Within 30 miles of Cass City, 125 families were sleeping the fields without any covering whatsoever, some being so stripped they were ashamed to show themselves, and have sent in one or two persons to obtain supplies for three or four naked families who are huddled together.

"Generous contributions continue to be made from this city in addition to those sent to the Board of Trade, Lumbermen's

54

Association and other organizations. Money from the firms here was sent liberally to Michigan."

Officials began calling for a relief effort that included lumber to rebuild houses, clothing, seed for future crops, bedding, and food.

Senator O.D. Conger of Port Huron and Port Huron Mayor E.C. Carleton led efforts to provide aid to their district.

One important American figure stepped in to help with relief efforts as she was recovering from health problems.

Clara Barton was lobbying the Congress and the Garfield Administration to sign the Treaty of Geneva and recognize the International Red Cross.

The American Red Cross was established on May 21, 1881. When Barton and others in her organizations heard of the Michigan disaster they set to work to provide relief – the first relief effort by the organization in America.

"Our relief rooms were instantly secured and our white banner, with its bright scarlet cross, was thrown to the breeze. ... We had not mistaken the spirit of our people; our scarce-opened doorway was filled with men, women and children bearing their gifts of pity and love. Tables and shelves were piled, our working committee of ladies took every article under inspection, their faithful hands made all garments whole and strong; lastly each article received the stamp of the society and of the Red Cross, and all were carefully and quickly consigned to the packing cases awaiting them," Barton wrote in remembering her agency's response.

Livingston County's County Clerk Mark Bunnell became the agency's point man for the disaster.

In New York City, a disaster relief committee set to work raising funds for the victims. The initial call was for $10,000 cash. That figure later would rise.

"A.J.D. Wedemeyer, a wholesale grocer, offered to gratuitously store all goods received and transport them to the railroad depot. W. E. Langley, connected with the New York Central Railroad Company, stated unofficially that the railroad would in all likelihood transport all goods contributed free of cost," The New York Times reported.

At a public forum at New York City's Chickering Hall the Rev. Robert Collyer, who went through the Chicago fire, called for the city to raise more than $100,000.

"He had been feeling keenly for the poor folk in Michigan, as one who had personally borne the pain and losses now suffered by sore affliction. The speaker's experience in the Chicago fire was one of unspeakable sadness. He saw his church and his home destroyed and his family without any other shelter than was afforded by a rude hut. … The reverend speaker thought that not $10,000 but $100,000 should be promptly and cheerfully raised for this purpose. He advised that church collections be taken up, that subscriptions be raised in every sewing society and that the businessmen everywhere make up their minds to contribute at least a little."

During the campaign to raise funds for the relief effort Michigan Lieutenant Governor James Birney visited the New York Stock Exchange and made at appeal for aid.

In Boston, the mayor of the city, asked for a meeting of merchants at City Hall. A Port Huron resident, C.G. Meisel, told the group that 10,000 people were in need of aid as the winter season approached.

"The situation is much worse than the newspapers have stated. The area of the burned district is 100 miles square. It was voted that a committee of seven be appointed to receive subscriptions and apply them as seems best in their judgment."

The president of the Boston Young Men's Christian Association donated $2,000. In San Francisco, the YMCA immediately raised $100 and vowed to send $500.

In Sarnia, Ontario, residents met to consider how to aid those across the lake. "Resolutions of condolence were passed and committees formed to solicit subscriptions. These are now at work and it is expected that a large sum will be raised."

The Tonawanda, New York, Lumbermen's Association sent $655 and in Goderich, Ontario, residents began to raise funds and collect bales of clothing and bedding.

The New York fundraising committee sent a representative to see the devastation. J.S. MacDonald, the group's secretary, sent back this telegram. His relatives lived in the devastated area:

"Have just emerged from the burned district. Have traveled over 75 miles of roads in it. The suffering and devastation is indescribable. In many places as far as the eye can see along the land once occupied by comfortable homes and a prosperous people, scarcely anything is visible but what seems a boundless sea of ashes, from which arises a stifling odor of burning flesh and bones. Blinded and fire-crazed people abound. Transportation is difficult, and supplies come through slowly, especially at a distance from the shore and by railway. A man is asked the whereabouts of his wife and children, and he stares wildly. He leaps at a loaf of bread and leaps away like a wild beast.

"Almost hourly the names of additional victims are added to the burned and to the death list. The homeless are thousands. The blinded, scorched, crippled, and deranged are very, very many. My own relations are heavy losers, but still have abundance and to spare for others. They are all alive, but my mother and brother will, I fear, lose their eyesight. Woeful want prevails, and will be hard to supply. For God's sake, let not the blessed hand of charity be too soon staid in New York."

By Sept. 18, the New York group had sent $33,300 in cash and packages of clothing and other materials. The New York Times reported that the soil would need to be regenerated.

"The devastation wrought by the fire has been such that the soil of the whole region is practically reduced to a condition of sterility that will endure for years. For the depth of more than one foot in some sections, the soil has been transformed into a layer of ashes by the intense and protracted heat, and its productiveness destroyed.

"The only remedy for this state of things is to turn up the deep and comparatively unburned subsoil and mix it thoroughly with the surface ash and debris. This is a work of time and toil, and one which, even when done, will but partially repair the destruction and infertility that have followed in the track of the fire. Many of the farmers owning property in the burned townships will probably find it better to abandon their long tilled acres and begin life anew in some more favored location, while others will attempt the rescue of their farms and rebuild as rapidly as they can obtain means."

Fund-raising continued in New York and the New York Central Railroad donated a space on the company's new pier for products to be sent.

English vocalist Leslie Main offered two musical lectures and vowed to send the proceeds to the relief effort. His Chickering Hall engagements featured a night devoted to "Alfred Tennyson" and another to "Poetry and Song."

On Sept. 16, Michigan Gov. Jerome issued a proclamation to the nation asking for help. In the proclamation, Jerome said the number of men, women and children without shelter was 15,000 and that the fires had claimed 200 lives and left many helpless through injuries.

"Entire neighborhoods are involved in the common calamity and cannot help each other. The sufferers have no provision except such as are brought from a distance and no utensils to cook with. The necessaries of life, both large and small, have been destroyed. They need shelter, clothing, shoes, cook stoves, kitchen utensils, beds and bedding, wagons, harness, plows, hoes, tools of all kinds, seed for future crops and whatever helps to make men self-supporting.

"Timely help will enable them to go through the coming winter and to become again an independent community. At present they are penniless, needy, sick and suffering. Many of them are in debt. The Governor asks the people of other states to cooperate in their abundance with the citizens of Michigan in relieving this destitution. Nothing will be in wanting here in duty to the afflicted sufferers; but the demands are too great for the people of the state to meet alone."

As people began to look at the fire, some light began to arise in the darkness. Those who endured the fire surely earned the titles of pioneer and survivor.

In the history, "Portrait and Biographical Album of Huron County," the authors compared the fire to Niagara Falls.

"It was as impossible to check this fire in its currents as to stem the Niagara. It swept over open fields faster than a horse could run. ... People speak of seeing blue flames shoot out from burning stumps, flicker a few seconds, and then be carried away with the wind. The air seemed to be heavily charged with gasses: there were literally balls of fire. ... We believe this fire has no parallel in the world's history. The Chicago fire of 1871 is the nearest approach to it."

But in every darkness and tragedy, the light arises – sometimes in unexpected ways. Despite some suggestions that the land was useless, farmers returned and started to do what they could with the ground.

Two weeks after the fire, the newspaper the Huron Times editorialized: "Prosperity will set in toward us stronger than ever, and our situation will be better than ever before ... Ten years from now Huron County will be millions richer. ... The curse of today will prove to be a blessing."

The fire cleared the land, making it more valuable for crops. In modern times, Huron County farmland boasts riches in beans, corn and sugar beets.

Many who endured the fire remained scarred physically and emotionally for the rest of their lives. Some dealt with the disaster with silence, carrying the loss of loved ones in their heart throughout the rest of their life and to the grave. Others somehow learned to cope. More than 10,000 were homeless and some 280 people were proven to have died. An exact death total was impossible to establish with many pioneers in the woods and new babies being born – even during the tragedy.

And then there was a young man named Charlie Hempstead who turned the tragedy into a new beginning for him and his intended.

The Detroit Post described the fiancée as the daughter of Mr. Nell of the Lakeview House somewhere near the village of Huron.

As the flames arrived, Miss Nell escaped but her family's home fell. Charlie suggested their wedding date be moved up and they begin a home of their own.

The Detroit Post Sept. 10 edition reported it this way: "With her consent they sought the house of a preacher midway between Huron City and Grindstone City when they were soon made man and wife. Her brother officiated as groomsman and Samuel Eckstein filled the kindly office of bridesmaid.

"On the way to the preacher's house they were obliged to run the horses for a mile through the fire, the scarf and dress of the expectant bride being scorched by the way. At Grindstone City, they were most kindly received and hospitably cared for till the arrival of the steamer, which was delayed till Thursday morning. About 20 others sought refuge at Grindstone City."

Today if one drives along the shore of Lake Huron on M-25 between Sebewaing and Bayport, a state historical marker gives an account of the tremendous loss and hardship Michigan pioneers endured.

The tragedy of the fire was overcome by the united efforts of many in the state and nation and those who suffered were suddenly more aware that the word "community" meant much more than what they previously thought.

Michigan Triumphs and Tragedies

Chapter Six
Tarzan's Papa stayed here

The jungles of Africa seem a long way from the shores of Orchard Lake.

However, imagination allows us to put the two together. And it could be that more than 100 years ago, a famous writer and novelist stood on the shores of the Oakland County body of water and pictured the rivers and lakes of Africa and the ape-raised man who swung through the vines.

One of the interesting stories of Michigan's literary history is the fact that Edgar Rice Burroughs, author of Tarzan, spent time at the well-respected Michigan Military Academy during the 1890s.

The academy was known for its strictness and discipline and the education that its students received. Many universities waived entrance exams for its graduates.

Started in 1874 by Capt. Joseph Sumner Rogers, a Civil War veteran, the academy became the leading military school outside of West Point for a time. Rogers was the drill instructor at Detroit High School when he got the idea to establish a military academy in the state. After its incorporation in 1877, graduates became lieutenants in the state militia.

The academy became the place to send sons for future military glory and it was a social coup for a belle of southern Michigan to be invited to a dance there.

Famous Civil War General William Tecumseh Sherman boosted the school's prestige by offering the school's first commencement address in 1879 and then in impassioned and impromptu remarks to the graduates afterwards warned them not to yearn to use their military prowess. He spoke about the wars he personally witnessed and the conclusion he had come to was that: "War is hell!"

Sherman now is best remembered for that quote.

How Burroughs got from the shores of Orchard Lake to the shores of the Dark Continent is a long story – almost as tangled as the jungle vines Tarzan used to swing through the jungle.

Burroughs was born in Chicago in 1875. His father, a Civil War veteran and successful businessman, wanted him out of Chicago during an influenza outbreak and sent him at 15 to live with his brothers on a ranch in Idaho. He experienced some of the remnants of the wild West and when his parents found out about it he was ordered to a military school in Massachusetts. The atmosphere there proved too confining for Burroughs and he ran away.

His father then sent him to the shores of Orchard Lake and Michigan Military Academy. Despite a rough start and trying to escape during the first year, he settled down and graduated in 1895. He was quarterback on the football team and editor of the newspaper.

He remembered the football glory in his unpublished biography.

"We had an unusually good prep school team, cleaning up everything in our class and a number of other teams that were out of our class. About the only teams that could beat us were such teams as Notre Dame and the University of Michigan, and at that we once held to a tie score the University of Michigan team."

Following graduation, Burroughs received an appointment to West Point, but flunked the mandatory entrance exam. He returned to Orchard Lake and taught geology, cavalry and Gatling gun to the cadets for half a semester before enlisting in the Army. He was assigned to the late Gen. George Armstrong Custer's 7th Cavalry.

The most famous Michigan Military Academy alumnus got bored in Arizona and with his dad's help left the Army after seven months and entered a series of jobs, including cowboy, merchant, salesman and police officer and struggled to find his place until he was in his mid-30s and wrote his first pulp fiction story. It sold for $400 and his new career was under way.

Burroughs wrote more than 20 Tarzan novels and published many science-fiction novels including "The Land That Time Forgot."

During World War II he served as a war correspondent. He died in 1950. His business acumen allowed him to become one the few successful authors who published himself and his works continue to bring in royalties today through Edgar Rice Burroughs, Inc.

The Military Academy operated for 30 years. For most of its existence it was in debt. Rogers died in 1901 and his brother tried to keep it going but it was closed in 1906 and the nine buildings sold to a church for a seminary.

Another noted graduate became a member of the nation's retail establishment. Sewell Avery led Montgomery War & Co. and John Christian Lodge, a dropout who spent six months at the school, later went on to fame as a Detroit politician and mayor.

In recent years, Burrough's ties to the Michigan Military Academy have been celebrated. Michigan residents can brag: "Tarzan's Papa once lived here."

Railroad tracks leading into Durand, Mich., site of the Wallace Bros. train wreck.

Chapter Seven:
Circus Becomes A Train Wreck

The Big Top became a big tragedy in Michigan early on August 7, 1903.

A train split into two sections, carrying the Wallace Brothers Circus of Peru, Ind., steamed along the Grand Trunk Line tracks northeast from Lansing. A stop at the railroad hub in Durand would be necessary before proceeding on the tracks northeast to a scheduled performance in Lapeer.

In the early Friday hours most performers and workers associated with the entertainment extravaganza tried to gain some sleep before another day of unloading, performing and then packing again.

The previous day's two shows in Charlotte went well with the usual routine of elephants, camels, horses and dogs. Acrobats, clowns and jugglers wowed the crowd.

The real crowd pleaser was Maud the baby elephant. The children especially enjoyed her entrance during the "elephant walk" as she paraded around the tent holding on to the tail of the bigger elephants in front of her with her trunk.

After the performance, the regular roustabouts and hired hands from the city went to work tearing down the canvas structures, packing the equipment, loading the train cars and then making the overnight run across the state. The sections left Charlotte shortly after midnight.

Owner B.C. Wallace knew his business and had become a millionaire by it. He knew how to spend and save a dollar. On his payroll were people from around the nation and Canada. There were hostlers, who cared for the horses, cooks for the employees, wagon drivers, a harness maker, blacksmith, canvas men responsible for the tents, members of the stake gang responsible for securing the tents and of course, the performers.

Many of the workers responsible for setting up and tearing down the tents, were fast asleep in the first section of the train as Engineer Schlyberlet slowed into the Durand yard at about 3 a.m. He was forced to stop the 21-car section because at the west end of the yard a freight train was coupling boxcars.

The rear brakeman immediately ran down the eastbound tracks a quarter-mile or so behind the caboose and set out a special lantern and lights called torpedoes to alert the second section of its predicament.

Inside the first section's caboose slept both railroad and circus employees.

Sleeping in bunks to one side of the car were James S. McCarthy, trainmaster with the Grand Trunk, A.W. Large, a railroad detective and Frank Thorp, the Wallace Brothers trainmaster.

On the other side of the car slept James F. Foley, a special officer with the railroad and J. Hazell of Battle Creek, a railroad foreman for locomotive engineers.

Schlyberlet had to keep his engine idling for 30 minutes until the stock train left the tracks. He then prepared to move onto the main line toward Lapeer.

Ahead of the caboose in the first section was a Pullman sleeping car where more than 40 of the behind-the-scenes workers slept. The car had been given to Wallace by the Chicago and Eastern Illinois railroad following a wreck that claimed two circus workers lives just three weeks earlier.

Meanwhile, as Schlyberlet idled in the Durand yards, Charles Propst, the engineer of the circus train's second section, kept the throttle open across the mostly flat country between Lansing and Durand. With him inside the cab of Engine 1133 were fireman H.E. Colter of Battle Creek and head brakeman, William Benedict of Durand.

The noise of the steam and huge pistons and roar of the boiler woke the sleepy forest around them as they made the run past the farm fields and forest toward the Durand yards, an intersection for railroad tracks in the state.

The warm August coupled with the heat of the locomotive boiler made Benedict drowsy. The new day promised as little sleep as the day before.

Behind the locomotive and tender with coal and wood for the engine's firebox was a boxcar carrying the elephants, including "Maud," and the four camels. The next car had horses and six circus workers responsible for the animals. In cars following were more horses and other performing animals and then in the last cars of the 16-car section the sleeping performers and circus officials.

Propst propped himself up in the seat and looked out beyond the noisy engine at the track ahead as he passed a marker indicating Durand ahead. The train negotiated a slight curve. He moved the throttle back slightly. He was traveling between 30 and 40 mph and knew he needed to slow down for the Durand yards. Suddenly, Colter yelled across the cab as the "stop" signals put out the brakeman on first train appeared. Benedict was now fully awake.

Propst immediately reversed throttle and pulled the air-brake lever. Nothing happened. He then whistled for brakemen to apply handbrakes. But he and the brakemen knew handbrakes on the cars were not functioning. Precious time was lost and the train's mighty mass shoved it forward quickly despite the backward churning wheels on the locomotive. The caboose of the first section loomed ahead. His train would not stop in time.

"Jump!" Propst screamed to the pair in the cab. Coulter and Benedict stepped to the side door opposite Propst and leaped into the darkness onto the grade and the westbound track. Propst knowing death lay ahead jumped from his side of the locomotive seconds before it plowed into the rear of the lamp-lit caboose.

Propst did not jump clean from the cab and ended up falling on his head, creating a bleeding gash. His nightmare was only beginning. Others would never awake.

The iron engine slammed into the oak-framed caboose at 20 to 30 mph with a deafening roar. Residents in the city woke from their sleep. The engine hit the caboose square in the back plowing into the sleeping men in their bunks. Hard oak sills eight-inches square from the caboose became sharp arrows as they penetrated into the boiler for 10 feet and the locomotive pushed the caboose forward and up off the tracks into the coach cars ahead. The momentum carried the caboose and the coaches off the tracks and then the engine itself up in the air.

The stack belching out steam somersaulted and landed on its side in the ditch, headed in the opposite direction. Its firebox spilled out coals.

Screams of wounded and dying workers mixed with the horror of terrified elephants, camels, horses and other animals in the mass of smoking debris.

The car carrying the five elephants and four camels behind the locomotive crashed into the coach of the first section where the foreman of the circus crew and his men slept.

Immediately the railroad men in the switchyard and others knew what happened. One man ran to the fire alarm and sounded it. The village soon came awake. Men appeared out of the darkness running down the tracks the half-mile outside of the city to where the collision occurred. An engineer and other employees jumped into a switch engine and headed down the westbound tracks that ran parallel to the eastbound.

At the end of the second train, G.E. Kies, a special agent with the circus awoke with the collision. He described what happened for reporters.

"I was riding in the second section, and was about 16

71

cars from the engine. It was just growing light in the east when I was awakened by a jolt that sent me ahead in the car. My first thought was that something had happened to the train and I dressed immediately. While I was getting on my clothes, one of the men who had been in the first section came running back toward our train and I asked him what happened. He told me everything was in a smash-up and that I had better get to the rear of the first section as soon as possible."[1]

When Kies ran to the front of his section, it was worse than he could have imagined.

"Many of the men who were badly injured were groaning and shrieking in misery, begging to be released. Just as soon as possible the alarm was given and everyone was awakened and the work of rescue began. Some of the men were dead when we took them from the wreck and others died soon after. Their cries of pain were terrible to hear."

The coach car immediately ahead of the caboose was demolished; others were telescoped off the tracks. Steam continued to blast out from the engine as it lay on its side. The tender rested on the other side of the tracks, completely blocking the line.

Job Naldrett, a village trustee, lived near the tracks on Oak Street. He lay half-awake in bed when he heard two shrill whistles from the second engine and then the crash. He grabbed his pants, shirt and vest, put them on and ran toward the sound. John Fauble arrived at the same time. Naldrett sent him into the village to get all the physicians.

Naldrett then tried to find his way into the rubble and

---

[1] The Durand Express, Thursday, August 13, 1903

pull people out. Many of the men he reached and untangled from the wreckage died in his arms.

Other people from the town started running up as well as circus workers.

"The Durand Express" newspaper describes what happened next:

"The cry, 'The wreck is on fire,' was one of the worst things that could have happened. It made the blood of the onlookers run cold, but just imagine how it must have sounded to the score of injured who were pinioned under the debris and were yet to be liberated. That alarm caused several of the afflicted to use inhuman strength in trying to pull away from whatever it was that held them and only added to their injuries. The alarm was false."

As the rescuers dug into the mass of debris, the scope of the tragedy became quickly apparent. In the caboose, Naldrett and others pulled out the bodies of McCarthy and Thorpe. They apparently died instantly. Their bodies were set to the side of the tracks and covered. Large, the detective, came out of the debris conscious enough to tell Naldrett that the hat found among the debris belonged to McCarthy. He was taken to the Hotel Richelieu. He died two hours later.

In the middle of the confusion and wreckage and screams the owner ran up from his train car. Naldrett saw Wallace break down into sobs. The scene was becoming too familiar, it was his second wreck in a month.

Foley and Hazell, who were sleeping on the opposite side of the caboose from those killed were thrown and buried under debris. They were injured but alive. Foley would later credit his life to a pack of playing cards in his vest pocket.

The cards were full of splinters and dented – apparently he was struck by a beam in the chest.

"It was all over so quickly there was no telling how it happened," he told a correspondent for the Detroit Free Press. "I was asleep at the time and the first thing I remember was being awakened when we were struck. The next second I was flying across the darkness and when it was over a heavy scantling lay across my foot in a manner that I was unable to free myself.

"The cries of the injured coupled with the bellowing of the animals was enough to make one's blood freeze in his veins. It was an experience such as I never want to pass through again.

"As soon as I recovered my senses I called out for help and a few minutes later they got the timbers off me so that they could pull me out. Then they brought me to town and here I am.

"Poor Large and McCarthy, they were right across the caboose from me, and I don't see how I ever managed to escape, while they were killed. I guess it would have put me out of business, too, if it hadn't been for that card case."[2]

Hazell was pulled unconscious from the debris and suffered injuries about his head.

A canvas man, Frank Tilly, of Rising Sun, Ind., also was quickly pulled out of the debris by rescuers. Three men in the car with him died shortly after the impact. He told rescuers two of the men were conscious enough to pray before they died. Someone offered Tilly some liquor. He refused and told the man he wanted to live a more godly life.

In all, 17 bodies were removed from the wreck. Others

---

[2] Detroit Free Press, August 8, 1903

lived only a short time.

A Durand Express reporter heard many of the injured point rescuers to others in more dire condition.

"Several of them would say, 'Get that fellow over there, I guess I am all right," the newspaper reported. "One man pulled himself out, walked over to the fence nearby, sat down and died in two minutes time."

As dawn arrived the full scope of the tragedy became more clear and bloody.

"Maud" and two camels were dead, another camel was injured and had to be shot. Apparently the baby elephant fell out or escaped from the tumbling box car it was in and then the car fell on top of it crushing it. The other elephants broke free of the debris and quickly ran over to a field where they were walking around and trumpeting.

Propst the engineer, stayed by the crash site. A Durand Express reporter spied him standing beside the body of McCarthy, the trainmaster.

"His face presented a bad sight, as it was torn and scratched by the cinders onto which he jumped. He was clearly much agitated and trembled like a leaf. He did not willingly grant an interview." The newspaper goes on to quote the engineer: "I saw the signals and knew the track was blocked. I attempted to stop the train, but the air would not work. That's all there is to it. I did all I could and did not leave the cab till I knew it as all up."

Later, Propst would testify that he had tested the air system when the train was in Lansing and it worked.

As soon as the wreck was known, the railroad put emergency plans into gear. A special train for the injured and more doctors were sent out of Detroit. Two railroad superintendents named McGuigin and Brownlee were dispatched to investigate the cause of the disaster.

After arriving shortly before noon they began their investigation. Their conclusion did not take long. They blamed Propst for the crash.

"We can control everything in railroading but the brains of our employees. And, too, when these men think they can work under their own ideas better than those of their superiors they make sad mistakes. This story of 'no air' is getting to be an old one," McGuigan told the Durand newspaper.

Crowds arrived from surrounding towns as the news of the disaster spread. Many brought their Kodak cameras. The circus as a tragedy was just as interesting a spectacle as the circus in performance. Wallace seeing little "Maud" ordered the dead elephant to be skinned on the tracks. He would have the skin sent to New York and be stuffed for promotional purposes.

A journalist tried to ask him about the wreck.

"Go and ask the railroad company what this wreck will cost," he replied.

The dead camels were to be buried. But many visitors were pulling hair and teeth from the dead creatures for souvenirs.

Ben Shultz took the job of skinning out "Maud" as the body of the creature lay on its back with its feet in the air beside the wreckage and in the middle of the growing crowd. Durand's Charles Deitchbuch wanted the tail for a souvenir. He took it home and boiled it for three hours and still was unable to stick a fork in it.

He boiled it nine hours the next day before finally being able to get the meat away from the bones. He reported: "The soup had a strong odor."

The railroad's doctors including Dr. R.C. Fair and Dr. Rowley worked without rest to do what they could for the injured as they waited for a special hospital train from Detroit that would carry the injured back to hospitals there.

The undertaker, G. W. McLain, called the wreck one of the most gruesome ordeals of his entire professional experience. He worked steadily on body after body performing embalmings at his mortuary.

Word was sent out by the railroad and circus to families of those who died. Bodies of victims were prepared for shipment to their hometowns, but it became apparent that many of the bodies remained unclaimed by family or friends.

On Aug. 9, a visitor arrived in Durand to hunt for his long-lost brother. He went down the line of corpses and then found his brother, William Griffin. He told officials he had not seen or heard from him in six years and asked that he be buried in the local cemetery.

Those uninjured in the wreck collected the undamaged circus gear and headed for Bay City for a show on Monday. Other competing circuses would lend equipment and personnel to ensure that the show would go on.

Meanwhile in Lapeer, 4,000 people who gathered to see the show Friday were disappointed and businessmen held a meeting to consider how to be compensated for promotions and preparations for the show.

Circus official J.O. Talbot first estimated the circus lost $5,000 for "Maud"; $1,000 for a performing Great Dane dog killed in the wreck; $1,800 for the three camels; $5,000 for the Arabian horse killed in the wreck and owned by bareback rider Owen Hollis; and $8,000 for its two railroad cars that were totally destroyed.

Later, Wallace estimated he lost $25,000 from the disaster, not counting the loss of revenue from the missed show dates.

The railroad kept trying to find relatives for the unclaimed bodies. A total of 23 people died in the wreck and 10 of the victims remained unidentified.

A funeral on the following Thursday for the unclaimed bodies involved most of the town. The Durand Express reported that businesses closed doors and a large crowd gathered along with singers from various churches in town who sang "Gathering

Site of the marker for the unclaimed bodies of circus workers in the cemetery south of Durand.

Home" and "It is Well With My Soul."

The Rev. Husted offered the appropriate words for the occasion and a C.E. Pickett read the scriptures. The Rev. J. McLean led a prayer. The bodies were buried in the Potter's Field within Lovejoy Cemetery.

Some of the circus employees quit following the wreck. Others stayed. Some of the injured told their stories:

"I was standing on the platform of one of the cars," Joe Anderson, a black, told a Detroit Free Press reporter at a hospital in Detroit. "I had a canvas over my head which covered me when I slept. I was pitched off the car, wound up in the canvas, dragged and hurt internally."

"My husband's scalp is terribly torn," said Mrs. Robert Abrams, of Geneva, Ill. She drove a chariot for the circus and her husband served as the "boss hostler" which meant he directed the care of the horses. "Mr. Abrams was buried in the caboose. He was lying inside the car that was on fire, but they put the fire out in time. One poor fellow picked up, gasped and died. The cars were piled up, everybody seemed crazy, and I am sure I did no know what I was doing myself."

"I am the lunch counter man," one victim told the Free Press. "When the crash came I went under the wheels and the trucks passed over me and broke one of my legs in two places."

One victim blamed the wreck on too many hunchbacks in the circus crew.

"Well, sir, I don't know how it happened that out of the three who escaped death in the last sleeper, two of us, Burt McGrath and myself, are fat men, but such is the case," said W.L. Cone, the circus steward. He back was sprained in the crash.

"We have two hunchbacks with us this trip and that is too many. Do I mean it? Of course I do. I am perfectly willing to admit that I am superstitious. I was sleeping in the upper berth near the rear end of the car and when the crash came the shock turned me over on my stomach and something began to shove me forward."

McGrath spoke out to defend the circus. He characterized the cars as well constructed.

"The cars were not old ones. They were two tourist sleepers give to Wallace by the Chicago and Eastern Illinois railroad in exchange for the sleeper that was wrecked at Shelbyville, but there is not a car in existence that could have stood the shock without going to pieces."

W.H. Howe, a circus driver, said: I was pinned down so I could not move. The wreckage above pressed in and nearly shut off my breath, and I was almost unconscious when I heard someone say: 'No use trying to get that on, he is all jammed to pieces.' Then though I was half dazed, I managed to wig wag with my boot and that brought help. And all I got was a good squeeze."

Even after the bodies were buried, a circus-like atmosphere continued in Durand. People began showing up wanting to claim a body and sue the railroad.

One man visited the town from Indianapolis, Indiana, and gave a description of who he claimed to be his son. When he was shown a photograph of a body, he immediately asserted it was his son.

In reality, the photograph represented a man named Charles McCoy, whose body was sent to his wife.

A coroner's jury was called to determine the cause of the disaster. The jury met August 14. Propst testified about the trip from Lansing, that he saw the warning signals, tried to apply the airbrakes and could not. He said he also whistled for handbrakes but none were functioning on the train.

A key question to him asked whether he had glanced at the air gauge on the trip from Lansing to Durand.

"No," Propst replied. He argued many engineers don't do that when they consider the engine functioning normally. Propst said previously he did have trouble with the air apparatus on No. 1133 and had reported it to the shop foreman in Port Huron. The apparatus was cleaned and reported back to be all right.

Propst told the jury where the air gauge was located in the cab. He agreed that because it was beside the steam valve, an engineer could see it all the time. In fact, he had to look past the air gauge to see the steam gauge. He also admitted that if had noticed the hands on this air valve anytime within a half-hour before approaching Durand, there would have been no wreck.

John Hazel, of Battle Creek, a traveling engineer for the railroad, testified he checked the air apparatus on the locomotive and everything seemed in working condition.

The jury adjourned to allow the actual mechanism to be inspected.

On August 27 the jury reconvened. Testimony showed the air brakes were in working order. Propst was called to the stand one more time. He stuck to his story about the air brakes.

"I would like to again state that I did everything to avoid that wreck that a man could have done. I know I did not look at the air gauge in my cab, but I made the run from the starting point to the time of the wreck just the same as ninety-nine out of a hundred engineers would have done, under the belief that everything was working all right."

After spending three hours in deliberation the jury returned and said the wreck was caused by the failure of the airbrake system and that its failure should have been noticed by Propst. The jury also blamed the circus for failing to provide proper hand brakes on its rail cars.

The conclusion: The wreck was unavoidable under those circumstances because the line was blocked.

The Grand Trunk railroad fired Propst.

Railroad veterans believe that he "lapped the brake valve" when he crossed tracks in Lansing. Many engineers did that to keep the speed slow and constant passing between tracks. If Propst forgot to reset the brake valve, he would have lost all of his air pressure before the wreck.

Today if you visit Durand, you can find the beautiful depot constructed in 1905 along with the double set of tracks still connecting the city with Lansing and other tracks headed northwest toward Port Huron and southeast to Detroit. The depot provides an office for Amtrak. One can see photographs from the circus train wreck and other railroad memorabilia at the railroad museum within the depot.

Southwest of town there remains a faded memorial in the Lovejoy Cemetery on Prior Road that honors the unclaimed bodies of the fateful wreck. There is also a faded little tombstone beside it with the words, "Unknown."

The memorial reads: "In memory of the unknown dead who lost their lives in the railroad wreck of the Great Wallace Shows." It then gives the wrong date: Aug. 6, 1903.

As you pull out onto the back roads about one-half mile from the town and look down the cornfields, along the tracks, one can still imagine that fateful morning a century ago. The names, the faces, the wailing of the elephants at the loss of Maud can almost seem real – just as it was on that day when the dawn brought disaster.

The Wallace Bros. Circus seemed to be plagued with railroad tragedies and despite two railroad disasters in 1903 there would come another more tragic wreck in the years ahead.

Chapter 7
The Great Storm
of 1913

Smoke belched out of the great stacks of the 504-foot steamer Charles S. Price as it churned past St. Clair on the St. Clair River northbound for Lake Huron.

On the shore, a young woman, gathered her coat about her. With expectant eyes she quickly searched the ship for a glimpse of her love. The huge boat was familiar and she was acquainted with many of the men on it. She had traveled the lakes with her husband earlier in the season. It was just after 6 a.m., Sunday, Nov. 9. Howard Mackley served as second mate on the Cleveland-based steamer. Florence Mackley, 26, had not seen him for a few weeks and hoped he would be coming home soon.

83

Her heart compelled her to be there. Early that morning she was bundled against the cold and waiting for her man, knowing the steamer left Cleveland the night before. Her long hair was pulled back in a bun and a colorful scarf protected her head and ears from the cold. A long, ankle-length dark wool coat hid her petite form from sting of the increasing wind.

The young couple married just the year before on June 26, 1912.

Outside the pilothouse, the second mate bundled his overcoat around his 5'8 frame and scanned the western shore of his hometown as St. Clair slipped by. It was always strange to be passing by family, friends and the city one knew so well, but unable to stop and even say "Hello." His father was a first-generation American in an English immigrant family. Howard was one of seven children. His family's farm was just a few miles away. Everything on shore was familiar, so familiar.

Everything on the ship was familiar as well. Too familiar. He was ready for the season to come to an end.

Suddenly on the shore, he spotted her, just as she spotted him. All they could do was wave. There was no sense in yelling, their voices would be drowned by the engine and the increasing wind coming from the southwest.

She loved him. He loved her. He wrote her a letter from Cleveland before the ship churned off telling her of his love and the fact that the ship picked up four new crewmen in Cleveland. One of the new hires replaced the boat's assistant engineer, Milton Smith.

Smith seemed such a level-headed guy, and then in Cleveland, he abruptly told the captain he was leaving the ship.

Smith told crewmembers that a vision of his wife and family pleading with him to come home seemed so real, that he could not ignore it. The vision gave him resolve despite the ridicule he knew he would get from some members of the crew. And the harsh words came, just as he expected.

Many on the ship questioned why he would leave the boat so late in the season and put a black mark beside his name with the Hanna shipping company. But Smith would not be dissuaded. He was determined to leave – and he did.

Deep down, Mackley understood, as he looked out at his own wife. Life on the lakes takes a toll on a man and his family.

The Price plowed on up the river for Port Huron. Mackley and his wife strained their arms in one last salute. She would never see him again.

At the wheel of the ship, Sidney Fennel, 25, of Detroit, kept a steady hand navigating the narrow passage. He was a lake veteran, despite his young age. He knew the pleasures of the lakes and its terrors. He survived the 1911 disaster aboard the steamer New York as it burned to the waterline in Thunder Bay. He and the rest of the crew barely got into lifeboats and pushed off before the fire consumed the boat. A steamer from the Pittsburgh line picked them up and took them to Detroit.

His family wanted him to quit the lakes, but he couldn't. It was in his blood. Now, he was on his way to Duluth. While the boat stopped in Cleveland, he sent a postcard to his brother Herbert, wishing him well. He hoped to see his family by Christmas. Captain W.A. Black, temporarily in his quarters, had warned Fennel to keep his eye on the weather.

Arze McIntosh, another wheelsman on the ship, was supposed to relieve him in a couple of hours. McIntosh's eyes were bothering him. Fennel took the night wheel.

Forecasters predicted some snow and high winds on the lake. But how can one predict a monster?

Yet, in a few hours, he, Mackley and 25 other crewmembers would be struggling in the jaws of something so brutal and terrifying that death must be the only result. Indeed, before the weekend was over, every sailor from Duluth to Buffalo would understand how puny man can be before the fury of wind and waves. Many prayers would be sent to heaven, many ships and sailors sent to the deep.

On Nov. 7, an Arctic air mass swept down from Alberta regions of Canada as a low-pressure system moved from plains into the Midwest. Behind the Arctic system temperatures were plunging into the single digits. Forecasters posted storm warnings for the lakes and predicted freezing weather would extend to the Florida and Georgia region.

As the two systems moved to collide over the Great Lakes area, a third low-pressure system developed over the Appalachian Mountains. It would track north-northwest and put it over Lake Huron and the monster low pressure systems would create ferocious winds, blinding snows, destroy telegraph wires and hurl the late season Great Lakes freighters around with waves of 30 feet and more.

Storm conditions started brewing late Friday in the western end of Lake Superior as the Arctic system entered the Upper Peninsula region on its way to Cleveland and Pittsburgh for a meeting with the Appalachian low system. The sting of snow and the whitecaps on Superior turned water to ice on the boats. Storm warnings signals were posted in the ports around the lakes. But the hurricane flags did not fly, something that many ship masters later would argue caused much of the lost of life.

On Lake Michigan, strong southwest winds pushing before the front changed to northwest after the front and waves began to pound Michigan's west coast. Boats docked in Holland, Ludington and Manistee were forced to stay put as rain turned to snow and wind speed increased to near 60 mph.

At the Soo Locks, boats continued to push through the locks both ways. Some ship masters hurried under pressure from headquarters to complete the last run of the season. They prayed to beat the weather into port and keep the owners happy.

From the western shore of Superior, the L.C. Waldo steamed out of Two Harbors, Minnesota, a port some 25 miles north of Duluth. Her cargo of iron ore set the 451-foot ship low in the water. By Friday night into early Saturday huge waves beat out a dirge as firemen down below struggled to keep their feet and feed the big boilers to keep up steam.

Rivets popping like bullets out of the hull told Captain John Duddleson the storm was not an ordinary gale and he needed to find shelter. He set a course for the Keweenaw Peninsula. As he and the wheelsman fought the waves to keep the propeller in the sea, it seemed the waves grew harder and faster by the minute. Both their feet kept sliding and they were forced to continually shift their balance to stand on the deck. Suddenly a wave rose up high above the ship and hit the pilothouse with a knockout punch, ripping it off the boat. Stung by the wash of cold water, Duddleson and his wheelsman instinctively scrambled back into a hatch. All was dark. The electrical power was gone.

Duddleson resorted to an auxiliary wheel and began steering by pocket compass and using a lantern for light. His reckoning with the little device in the blinding snow and raging tempest proved fairly accurate. The ship almost made the passage between Manitou Island and Keweenaw Point. Near 3 a.m. in the morning, the captain could hear the waves hitting the rocks of the island. But he could not turn the big ship fast enough in the wind and waves. The bow plowed ashore on the west end of the island. Waves pounded his ice-coated stern.

Duddleson ordered all hands into the forepeak of the ship to wait for the end. Two women who were part of the crew cowed in the galley area. They were escorted topside and two men of the crew literally carried the women across the ice covered deck as waves tried to wash them away.

The crew fashioned a bathtub into a fire pit and started burning wood and anything else for warmth.

By Sunday a report made its way on the wire from the Upper Peninsula to points south.

"An unknown steamer has been on the west end of Manitou Island near Gull Rock lighthouse since late Friday night and was reported at Bete Gris this morning by the George B. Stevenson, which made ineffectual attempts to reach her. The Eagle Harbor lifesavers tried for 12 hours to get to Manitou, but each time they crept out from the lee of the point they were swept back by the fierce northeast gale, which blew 70 miles per hour. The Stevenson reports the wreck lying low, with decks almost awash and every wave breaking over here cabins and masts. They counted 28 men on the decks or lashed to the rigging, several of them evidently dead from exposure."

The report about the dead and being lashed to rigging was not true.

The crew, cold, wet but very much alive held on as waves tried to break the ship apart below them. By Monday the Captain Thomas McCormick of the Portage rescue station, reached the wreck of the Waldo. Captain Charles A. Tucker brought a tug from the Eagle Harbor station and together they rescued all 24 crewmembers. As the crew was being rescued Monday, a fisherman at Big Bay, 40 miles south of Manitou Island, found wreckage of the Waldo's pilothouse and other parts of the ship bearing its name.

Another ship trying to make its way through Superior also ran aground early Saturday. The Turret Chief crew abandoned ship after the ship was pushed on the rocky Keweenaw Peninsula coast just 5 miles east of Copper Harbor. Once on shore, waves and snow covered them. There was nowhere for the soaked sailors to go for shelter except to try and find an overhang or shelter from the wind. Their clothes were stiff with ice and their matches would not light. There was nothing to eat from Saturday to Monday morning. Monday, Indians came to the rescue. Native Americans arrived in single file and led them into Mandan.

Another steamer, the Henry B. Smith left Marquette Sunday afternoon despite the rough conditions. The 525-foot Smith carried 9,000 tons of iron ore. Despite waves washing over the breakwater, Captain James Owen reportedly joked about the gale. He arrived late in port and apparently felt he needed to make up for lost time. As soon as the last ton of iron ore was aboard he signaled his departure. The 32 hatches on the ship were not yet secure.

Some of the old salts in Marquette had their mouths open as the ship steamed out of the port and into the fury of the lake.

89

The ship disappeared from view after 20 minutes. Some time after that Owens and his crew disappeared into eternity.

On land, the blizzard of wind and snow swept across Michigan and the U.S. east of Chicago snapping telegraph lines and creating havoc with all manner of transportation. Temperatures in Pittsburgh fell from 48 degrees to 22 degrees in less than 15 hours. Ten inches of snow piled up in drifts. The Appalachian low met the Arctic and other low and fed into a monster system. The barometer dropped to 28.60 inches.

The intimidating weather mass tracked from Pittsburgh across Erie and toward Lake Huron as Sunday dawned and progressed.

By Sunday afternoon, telegraph operators in Detroit could not get through to Cleveland, Toledo, Buffalo or other parts of the lake. There was a slow line still available to Sault Ste. Marie. The news from there soon became worrisome and then tragic as the Arctic low did its toll on the fleet and wind speeds grew and changed as storm fed each other.

"We never had a letup from the time we left Duluth," reported Capt. Story of the steamer Maricopa after making the Soo Locks on Sunday. "The gale blew 50 mph all the way down Superior. The ice gathered fast on our boat. It was necessary at times to thaw it away from the front of our wheelhouse in order to see. The furious wind, coupled with the freezing temperatures made it one of the fiercest trips I have made for years."

Capt. Neil Campbell of the Sarnian also made the Soo on Sunday after a long trip across Superior from Thunder Bay, Ontario. He called the storm the worst he had ever encountered in 25 years of sailing the lakes.

The old iron ore dock in downtown Marquette where the Henry B. Smith possibly loaded on its last voyage.

Photo courtesy of Michigan Technological University Archives and Copper Country Historical Collections

The steamer "Turret Chief" is wrecked on the rocks on the Keweenaw Peninsula in November 1913.

"We left Port Arthur (Canada) Tuesday at midnight. My barometer was falling, but the wind had not sprung up yet. When I got around Thunder Bay cape it began to blow from the southwest. I saw my boat could not make it with wind from that direction, so I went back behind the cape.

"Five times I made the effort to get out. It was not until Wednesday night that I got started. Thursday brought me as far as Jackfish and I laid under the bluffs there until Friday night. I saw the lights of Mission Point Saturday night. I was forced to find an anchorage behind Michipocoten Island which I left this morning. It was blowing hard with snow from the northeast as I came down. I could see two or three boats trying to make their way up, but I think they came back. A big fleet hugged the south shore of Whitefish Bay as I came by."[1]

As it turned out, Campbell did not realize how fortunate he was. About 50 steamers were reported anchored between Sault Ste. Marie and White Fish Point.

Capt. Balfour of the steamship The Barry regarded the storm as something to be feared. His ship headed north on Sunday and the wind and waves pushed him back.

"This is the first time I ever lost an anchor by letting it go. The wind was something terrific. We were laying under Whitefish Point when the wind took a turn to the northeast and north so quickly that before we could meet it our anchor chains snapped and we had to turn around."

Damage reports began arriving in Detroit from Milwaukee and Chicago: Two men were blown into the river and drowned in the Windy City. Wind and waves undermined its pier and

---

[1] Detroit Free Press, November 10, 1913, Page 2

pilings. A coal boat off Waukegan bucked in the waters off the

coast, unable to dock because of the waves. Milwaukee piers and ships were damaged by the storm. In Holland, the steamer D.C. Perry was blown from its moorings onto the beach. The storm damaged homes, the pier and the interurban track.

The storm arrived as the shipping industry prepared to tally a record-breaking season of lake traffic. Tons of coal, iron ore, copper, lumber and grain, limestone and sugar were weighted down within the holds of the massive freighters.

Now the cargo and the sailors were held captive by a storm bent on destruction.

As the storm progressed some 20 ships or more sought shelter off Alpena in Thunder Bay. In the Detroit and St. Clair rivers more than 40 ships set anchor and tried to escape the winds. Captains didn't dare to try and navigate the narrow channels with such a small room for error and the wind looking for opportunity to blow their mammoth ship to shore.

One steamer, the "Pollock" couldn't maintain her course in the winds and the ship became mired in the St. Clair Flats, an area where the St. Clair River enters Lake St. Clair. A tug sent to rescue the Pollock was unable to do anything because of the high winds

Another steamer, the Wauketa arrived in Detroit unable to make most of its scheduled stops in the Flats because of the blinding snow. A giant swell on Lake St. Clair forced in one of the gangways of the ship.

Steamers from Detroit to Cleveland were canceled.

In Port Huron, 15 ships that set out northbound on the lake earlier Sunday returned to try and find shelter on the St. Clair

River. The Charles S. Price was not among them. Snow and winds were piling drifts on the shore.

U.S. Lightship 61, stationed north of the St. Clair River, was hurled ashore early in the big wind. The steamer Matthew Andrews, down bound with a load of iron ore, saw the lightship and put down anchor thinking the lightship was in place. The boat was driven by waves into the Corsica Shoals.

Capt. A.C. May on the H.B. Hawgood, sighted the Price north of Harbor Beach. The ship labored in heavy seas. May decided to turn his vessel back. On the way he met the upbound Regina 15 miles south of Harbor Beach and at 3:30 p.m. saw the Isaac M. Scott five or six miles north of Gratiot Light. He was the last to see those boats afloat.

The long, cold blustery night on shore Sunday was nothing compared to the terror of the angry tempest battering every rivet, latch, window and weakness on the boats shuddering and shivering on the lonely white darkness of the lakes.

In Port Huron on Monday, the steamer H.W. Smith limped into port. The boat was covered with ice and the crew exhausted, hungry and cold, but thanking God for delivering them through the worst ordeal of their lives.

The ship Sunday had passed through Port Huron headed for Milwaukee with a load of coal from Buffalo. As it neared Saginaw Bay, the storm blanketed them with a vengeance as fierce as any enemy in ambush. Sailors described waves breaking over the entire boat.

The pounding of the terrible waves became as hard as giant fists, knocking out the windows of the pilothouse and creating destruction on all parts of the boat.

95

During the night, porter Paul Becker, dared going outside to get some coal for a stove. A huge wave swept him down the passageway against the fan-tail of the steamer. He was rescued just before another wave would have swept him overboard. Both legs were badly injured.

The steamer's steward, John F. Sweeney and his wife, also employed on the boat, arrived with serious injuries.

Across Lake Huron on the Canadian side, the steamer, The Wexford, was trying to make its way to shelter at Goderich. The 270-foot package freighter officially was last seen 35 miles north of the Canadian port and was under the command of Master Bruce Cameron. Some reported a glimpse of masts off Goderich in midafternoon during the fury of the storm.

Other ships on the lake included the James C. Carruthers, the Hydrus, The African Queen, the Argus and the J. H. Sheadle.

Just north of Port Huron at the Lakeview lifesaving station, Captain Plough on Monday spotted the hull of a ship sticking out of the water. But there was nothing he could do. Winds gusting 60 mph and five feet of snow destroyed his boats and his boathouse. As he studied the sight, his only conclusion was that all hands must be lost. When a tugboat finally was sent the next day, the name of the ship could not be identified.

Reports of more problems began arriving across the telegraph wires that remained working.

At Thunder Bay, the 300-foot Acadian was reported grounded and taking on water. The ship carried a load of cement and wire.

Reports arrived of boat aground at Angus Island in Superior and men clinging to decks. A sand steamer north of Belle Isle collided with a steamer.

Bad news and destruction grew worse as the hours passed.

Lake Huron waves on Monday carried eight bodies onto the shore of Canada some eight miles from Port Huron. Some of the lifejackets and other wreckage seemed to identify they were the crew of the 249-foot-long steamer Regina that was trying to go north out of Sarnia, Ontario. At the time of the disaster the ship was trying to make Harbor Beach with a load of package freight. Then the ship's freight started to wash ashore in Canada as well. A lifeboat with the name "Regina" was found on the Canadian shore and the bodies of two men inside the lifeboat. In all there were 10 bodies and most wore life preservers.

The mystery of the overturned boat near Port Huron continued on Tuesday. Its black bottom confounded many mariners who thought the ship could be the Regina. The Regina's hull was green.

Meanwhile, Florence Mackley along with other wives of crews waited anxiously for news.

The Price's assistant engineer Milton Smith arrived home to St. Clair telling friends and reporters that he had a premonition of the disaster. He felt terrible about the likely fate of his friends on board the ship.

"I am sorry for poor Arze McIntosh of St. Clair, our wheelsman. When Arze heard that I was coming back to Port Huron he came up to me and and said, "Milt is it true that you are going to leave the ship?"

"I told him that it was, and he said, 'Well, I wish that I was going with you. I can see poor Arze now. The boy was having troubled with his eyes and wanted to come home to have them operated on. He practically had made up his mind to come along with me, but said that he guessed that he would stick it out for just one more trip."[2]

Meanwhile at Port Austin, rescuers led by the oldest rescuer on the lake finally reached the steamer the Hanna and pull off the crew of 18. The crew spent 48 hours on the ship.

Capt. Henry Gill of the Port Austin rescuers overcame many obstacles to get the crew off the ship. When the distress signal was given after the boat was spotted Sunday night off the coast, Gill and others in his rescue station could do nothing. Winds and waves wrecked their boathouse and dock and their surfboat was buried in the sand and snow.

The Hannah had passed up the St. Clair River just ahead of the Price and passed Harbor Beach at 11:30 a.m. But by 2 p.m. at Port Aux Barques, at the tip of the Michigan Thumb, the ship's crew fought for control of the boat and then for their lives. The seas pounded the ship mercilessly, demolishing the pilothouse and taking the starboard lifeboat. The Captain saw the light at Port Austin but the ship became grounded and then waves proceeded to break it in two.

On shore Monday morning, rescuers found a lifeboat, put it on a wagon and launched it about a mile north of their lifesaving station.

The lake and winds threatened their own lives. By the time their boat had made most of the journey to the Hannah, their own craft hit a rock and started taking on water. They had to turn back – barely making it back to shore in the battered craft.

Calls to rescuers at Harbor Beach and Huron City were fruitless. Each had wrecks they were dealing with.

---

[2] Detroit Free Press, November 14, 1913

With their battered lifeboat useless, the men started digging the surfboat out of the sand. Finally at 8 p.m. Monday the boat was dug out and patched enough to try a second rescue attempt.

Tuesday morning they launched and met seven of the Hanna's crew trying to make shore in the ship's yawl boat. The rescuers proceeded to the Hanna and took six men and woman off and then rowed back to shore.

They then went back to the Hanna and removed the rest of the crew, including the captain.

A letter written by one of Gill's daughters recounted how townspeople waited on shore with hot coffee. And those rescued and the rescuers were taken to the hotel for a hot meal. Among those taken off the ship was an unidentified woman wearing men's socks, a man's shoe and moccasin and suffering from hypothermia.

At the Soo, word arrived that two steamers were grounded on Sand Island on the Canadian side of Superior just opposite Whitefish Point. The Hartwell and The Hutchinson both were taking on water. The crew of The Hartwell was able to keep up steam in the engine room to stay warm. Its engine room and quarters area remained dry.

The steamer the William Nottingham also was discovered on a reef between Sandy Island and Parisienne in Whitefish Bay. Crew of the grain freighter tried to lower a boat and get help earlier, but a wave overturned the small craft as it lowered down to the sea. Three sailors were lost.

By Wednesday, mariners in Marquette worried as there was no report of the Henry B. Smith making the Soo locks. Some start to question the captain's decision Sunday afternoon to head into the teeth of the storm.

In Port Huron Thursday the body of the C.S. Price's engineer John Groundwater was found on shore wearing the lifejacket from the steamer Regina. Officials began to speculate that the Price and Regina collided and wondered if the overturned steamer with the black hull could be the Price. Other members of the Price's crew had Regina lifejackets in their hands when their bodies washed up on shore.

Maybe the Regina was underneath the Price?

Smith, the former price assistant engineer, headed for Canada with authorities and identified bodies from his ship.

Florence Mackley also made the trip with her two sisters. She immediately recognized Groundwater and the steward, Jones. Her husband's body was missing and would never be found. Smith tried to help her in her search.

By Friday a tugboat and diver dispatched to the mystery ship uncovered the name of the boat. It was the Charles S. Price. No other ship was underneath and the mystery of how the bodies of both the Regina crew and Price crew mixed puzzled many.

More bodies washing ashore on the Canadian beaches provided a gruesome task for Canadian farmers. One woman was found ashore wearing the captain's life jacket. Two sailors were found clasping onto each other.

In the middle of the storm and continuous reports of loss, The Detroit Free Press accurately penned the historical significance of the storm. It was that awesome and the journalists knew it.

On Nov. 14, 1913, the Free Press reported: "The chapters of the greatest tragedy of the Great Lakes are now being written. It is a story of successive tragedies without parallel in fresh water maritime annals. Each hour, in fact, each message that comes clacking over the wires adds to the horror of the situation ad when the end mark is written there will be a monetary loss to the shipping of the lakes that will run into the millions."

Some two weeks after the storm, the body of one of the crewman of the Henry B. Smith was found floating in a lifejacket some 50 miles west of Whitefish Point. Wreckage from the boat was found near Grand Marais: A single oar, a ladder with the name "Henry B. Smith," a piece of deckhouse and two cabin doors.

The following May, the decomposing body of ship's chief engineer John Gallagher was found washed on the shore of Michipocten Island.

Another eerie discovery following the storm involved the barge, the Plymouth, in Lake Michigan near St. Martin's Island. A tugboat had been pulling the barge but took on water and left the barge anchored in raging waves while it went ashore to pump out. When it came back the barge and the seven men on it were missing without a trace. One of the men on board was U.S. Marshal Chris Keenan. He was custodian of the barge and his body later washed ashore near Manistee. About 10 days later, a bottle washed ashore near Pentwater. It was a note from Keenan to his family.

His message was simple and straightforward:

"DEAR WIFE AND CHILDREN:

WE WERE LEFT UP HERE IN LAKE MICHIGAN BY MCKINNON CAPTAIN JAMES H. MARTIN, TUG AT ANCHOR. HE WENT AWAY AND NEVER SAID GOODBYE OR ANYTHING TO US. LOST ONE MAN YESTERDAY. WE HAVE BEEN OUT IN STORM 40 HOURS. GOODBYE DEAR ONES, I MIGHT SEE YOU IN HEAVEN. PRAY FOR ME.

CHRIS K."

Looking back on the disaster, it still ranks as the worst maritime disaster in the lakes. The event became a historic marker for many Great Lakes sailors. The question became, "Where were you during the big blow of November 1913?"

At the end of their careers in the mid-1950s, three maritime veterans told the Sault Ste. Marie, Ontario, Sault Daily Star newspaper the storm was something they never forgot.

Longtime harbormaster at Sault Ste. Marie, Frank Parr recalled he was on a ship headed for Marquette when the gale arrived.

"I was a passenger aboard the Winona going to Marquette and in 36 hours we made a distance of eight miles. Needless to say, I returned by rail."

Capt. E.F. Raeburn recalled the storm as a crewman aboard the City of Chatham off Thessalon, Ontario, in the North Channel above Drummond Island.

"All of a sudden, Lake Huron seemed to go back into the North Channel and the boat settled down in the water. My room aboard ship had a foot of snow in it, but at that we fared better then hundreds of others that night."

Capt. J.W. Alexander was just a 16-year-old wheelsman on the Thomas J. Drummond when he met the worst storm of his entire lake career.

"It was the night of Nov. 11 and that gale was the worst ever. Our ship passed the Palaki off Whitefish Point and I guess we were the last to see her."

Capt. S.A. Lyons of the J.H. Sheadle was one of the few to survive the storm and travel the length of Huron from top to bottom as other ships were going down. His ship took a beating but won the fight against the weather giant. He passed

down, bound from Superior into Lake Huron with the James
Carruthers ahead of him and the Hydrus behind him. Both the
Carruthers and Hydrus would go to the bottom of the lake. He
saw the Carruthers taking on fuel at Thunder Bay in Alpena. It
was probably the last view of that ship.

He continued south toward Port Huron and the St. Clair
River and ran into the jaws and claws of the weather monster.
Like the other captains of the 18 ships battling Lake Huron
Sunday and early Monday, he was unaware of the severity of the
blow when he left Sault Ste. Marie.

"While the barometer was low and the high northwest
winds were scheduled, there was nothing to indicate either in the
sea or the wind at that time that the passage could not be made
with reasonable safety."

Here is part of an account of his trip first published in the
March 1914 "Marine Review." The excerpt begins after the boat
traveled south across Lake Huron to the Pointe Aux Barques at
the tip of the Thumb:

> "We got regular soundings at Pointe Aux Barques
> that we had been getting on previous trips, and by
> the soundings and the time we could tell when we
> were abreast of the Pointe. It was snowing a
> blinding blizzard and we could not see anything.
> According to the soundings we got by the deep
> seas sounding lead we were abreast of Harbor
> Beach at 4:50 p.m., and three miles outside the
> regular course we take during the summer. At this
> time the wind was due north and at Harbor Beach

we changed our course to due south running dead before the sea and wind.

"The bell rang for supper at 5:45 p.m., which was prepared and the tables set, when a gigantic sea mounted our stern, flooding the fantail, sending torrents of water through the passageways on each side of the cabin, concaving the cabin, breaking the windows in the after cabin, washing our provisions out of the refrigerator and practically destroying them all, leaving us with one ham and a few potatoes. We had no tea or coffee. Our flour was turned into dough. The supper was swept off the tables and all the dishes smashed.

"Volumes of water came down on the engine through the upper skylights, and at all times there were from 4 to 6 feet of water in the cabin. Considerable damage was done to the interior of the cabin and fixtures. The after steel bulkhead of the cabin was buckled. All the skylights and windows were broken in. A small working boat on the top of the after cabin and mate's chadburn were washed away.

"It was blowing about 70 miles an hour at this time, with high seas, one wave following another very closely. Owing to the sudden force of the wind the seas had not lengthened out as they usually do when the wind increases in the

104

ordinary way. In about four hours the wind had come up from 25 to 70 miles an hour, but I do not think exceeded 70 miles an hour.

"Immediately after the first sea swept over our stern, I ordered the boatswain to take sufficient men and shutters to close all windows in the after cabin. They forced their way aft, braving the wind, sleet and seas, one hand grasping the life rail and the other the shutters. Reaching the after cabin in safety, they began securing the shutters, when another tremendous sea swept over the vessel, carrying away the shutters. The men were forced to cling to whatever was nearest them to keep from being washed overboard; immediately a third sea, equally as severe, boarded the vessel, flooding the fantail and hurricane deck.

"The men attempted to reach the crews dining room, but could not make it, and only saved themselves by gripping the nearest object they could reach, indeed one of the wheelsmen was only saved from going over by accidentally falling as he endeavored to grope his way to the rail, his foot catching in one of the bulwark braces, preventing him from being swept off. Another monster sea boarded the boat, tearing the man loose from the brace and landing him in the tow line, which had been washed from its after rack and was fouled on the deck.

"The men finally made the shelter of the dining room and galley. One of the oilers stood watch at the dining room door, closing it when the boat shipped a sea and opening it when the decks were clear to let the water out of the cabins."

Through the captain and crew's seamanship the Sheadle survived the 16-hour storm with its load of wheat. They fought the waves until Monday at 2 a.m. when the storm system's worst was over and his boat could navigate without fear of the huge wave troughs.

The Lake Carrier's Association Report on the storm called it one for the centuries:

"No lake master can recall in all his experience a storm of such unprecedented violence with such rapid changes in the direction of the wind and its gusts of such fearful speed. Storms ordinarily of that velocity do not last over four or five hours, but this storm raged for 16 hours continuously at an average velocity of 60 miles per hour, with frequent spurts of 70 and over.

"Obviously with a wind of such long duration, the seas that were made were such that the lakes are not ordinarily acquainted with. The testimony of the masters is that the waves were at least thirty-five feet high and followed each other in quick succession, three waves ordinarily coming one right after another.

"They were considerable shorter that the waves that are formed by the ordinary gale. Being of such height and hurled with such force and such rapid succession, the ships must have been subjected to incredible punishment.

"Masters also relate that the wind and sea were frequently in conflict, the wind blowing one way and the sea running in the opposite direction. This would indicate a storm of cyclonic character. It was unusual and unprecedented and it may be centuries before such a combination of forces may be experienced again."

The storm has been compared to the more modern blizzard of January 1978 when a massive snowstorm blocked Interstate 75, shut down factories and airports and stranded people around the state. That storm also involved an Appalachian low that fed off an Arctic low from Canada.

After the 1913 disaster, a congressman from Cleveland asked President Woodrow Wilson to investigate the weather service and the warnings that were issued. The weather service denied it was at fault.

Since 1847 there have been 25 killer storms on the Great Lakes. There is no dispute that the 1913 disaster took the heaviest toll of both ships and sailors. Some 254 sailors drowned or froze to death and 12 ships sank. Seven ships were extensively damaged and 18 ships ran aground.

At least five bodies that floated ashore in Canada were never identified and buried at a cemetery in Goderich, Ontario. A marker above the bodies gives tribute to the sailors who died in the storm.

Most of the freighters lost in the storm have been found and offer interesting diving. The Wexford was just discovered in

2000 and is in 65 feet of water 11 miles southeast of Michigan's Lexington Harbor in Ontario waters sitting up on the bottom.

Here is a listing of the boats sunk and the men lost and where the boats rest if known:

- John A. McGean of Cleveland with a crew of 19 originally thought lost off Sarnia. The ship was discovered off Port Hope upside down in 185 feet of water.
- Charles S. Price of Cleveland with a crew of 20. Lost between Lakeport and Port Huron. The boat is upside down in 70 feet of water.
- James S. Carruthers of Toronto with a crew of 22. Some of its wreckage washed ashore at Grand Head, Ont., beside Lake Huron. The boat has not been found.
- The Regina of Toronto with a crew of 20. It capsized in Lake Huron possibly in the vicinity of the Price and was discovered in 1986 between Lexington and Port Sanilac.
- The Wexford of Toronto with a crew of 20. Lost off the Canadian shore south of Goderich, Ontario. Discovered in 2000 resting on the bottom in 65 feet of water south of Goderich, Ontario.
- The Leafield of Sault Ste. Marie, Ont. Crew of 15 lost at Angus Island, Lake Superior. Boat never found.
- Plymouth of Menominee, Mich., with a crew of seven. Sunk off St. Martin's Island in Lake Michigan. Barge never found.

- Lightship No. 82, with a crew of six, sunk off Buffalo in Lake Erie.
- William Nottingham, three of crew of 25 drowned, wrecked near Sand Island, Lake Superior.
- Henry B. Smith, crew of 18. Lost somewhere between Marquette and Whitefish Point in Lake Superior. Boat never found.
- The Hydrus, crew of 23. Lost somewhere in northern Lake Huron. Boat never found.
- The Argus, crew of 24, located in 225 feet of water.

There is a Michigan historical maker along the highway overlooking Lake Huron that reminds state residents of the storm. It reads:

"Sudden tragedy struck the Great Lakes on November 9, 1913, when a storm whose equal veteran sailors could not recall, left in its wake death and destruction. The grim toll was 235 seaman drowned, 10 ships sunk, and more than 20 others driven ashore. Here on Lake Huron all 178 crewmen on the eight ships claimed by its waters were lost. For 16 terrible hours gales of cyclonic fury made man and his machine helpless."

The Italian Hall in Calumet the day following the Dec. 24, 1913, disaster.
The doorway leading to the second-floor hall is at left.

CHAPTER 9
ITALIAN HALL DISASTER

Toothy grins and wide eyes of anticipation showed the excitement and pleasure unfolding in the second-floor auditorium of the Italian Hall on 7th Street in Calumet. It was late afternoon on Christmas Eve, 1913.

A brightly decorated evergreen sat on the right of the stage and in chairs on the left side presided members of the Calumet Women's Strike Auxiliary. They wore their Sunday dresses. The grins belonged to the children in the crowded hall as they watched a Christmas program carefully planned and executed by the women as a way to introduce happiness into a season of hardship and struggle for mining families.

Inside the crowded hall the 700 spectators watched special skits and dances. They sang carols. A few mothers cradled their infants and one of the fathers sat with his young daughter on his lap. Almost everyone there belonged to the Western Federation of Miners and was living day to day as the union continued its strike against the Calumet and Hecla Mining Co. The strike began in July.

Throughout the late summer and fall the union staged parades in the mining villages to show the solidarity of those who worked deep in the copper mines. Strikers wanted shorter workdays, better pay, safer working conditions, the elimination of a new tool call the one-man drill and respect from the mine owners for their union.

The owners responded by bringing in more immigrant workers and sending them down the shafts to drill out the copper ore. An organization of townspeople formed a group called the Citizen's Alliance to show their support for the mine owners. The miners on strike represented different nationalities including Finnish, Croatian, Italian, Slovenian and Swedish.

Copper country in the Keweenaw Peninsula had long boasted the number one source of copper for the world, but mines in Arizona and Montana also supplied a lot of the nation's need for copper as well.

The strikers in Calumet were part of the socialist labor movement that also was sweeping the coal regions of West Virginia and Kentucky, the gold mines of Colorado and other mining regions in the West and Northwest. With the strikes came violence. In the Keweenaw Peninsula, Michigan's Gov. Woodbridge Ferris had dispatched the National Guard to keep the peace and protect public property.

The mining company hired a detective agency from New York to protect its property and interests. And in the course of events preceding the Christmas season there had been deaths on both sides of the strike.

112

But politics and the miners' agenda were all put aside for Christmas Eve. The ladies, led by Anna Clemenc, nicknamed "Big Annie" for her role in helping organize strikers and call attention to the needs of miners, just wanted the children to enjoy themselves and experience an oasis in the middle of their families' jobless struggle against the winter. Big Annie had spent time in jail for her strike involvement.

As the celebrants arrived at 7th Street, they entered a doorway on the left side of the building that led to the bottom of a set of stairs. Union members checked each person attending for a union card. Those who did not have one were turned away or had to find another union member to vouch for them.

Once entry was approved, celebrants climbed the 21 stairs that led up to a landing and then through double doors on their right they entered the hall. The hall was built in 1908 and boasted a balcony that ran along the south side of the building. There was the big stage and a kitchen in an area beneath the stage, separate toilets for men and women and a ticket room that could be entered from the stair landing or the hall.

The program began with Christmas carols sung in English. Following the songs, a young boy recited a special reading for the occasion. The audience applauded. A Finnish man got up to speak and the 500 children tried to stay still in their seats. All were wearing their best clothes. Then it was time for a group of Croatian adults to dance and sing. The crowd enjoyed watching the performers.

Following the dancers a group of children sang. Annie noticed the children were growing restless. They decided to cut out a skit and get to the main event. All the children were

113

directed to line up along the north wall of the 78 foot-long hall and parade onto the stage.

On walked Santa to the delight of all the children in the hall. He carried a bag with goodies for all the children. There were squeals of delight and some shoving as they anticipated a small gift. The noise from the children in the balcony and on the floor filled the hall as they hurried into line. Some children were directed back into their seats.

One by one boys and girls started filing past Santa for a special gift. Those who received their gift were directed through a series of doors and corridors that would take them off the stage and back into a kitchen area and around the hall so it would be difficult for them to just run back in line for another present.

Some children left after receiving their gifts.

But passing out gifts for 500 children would take time. The hundreds of children squealed and the noise in the hall rose. Annie shouted for the children to be silent and directed more of them to sit in the front seats near the stage. The curtain on the stage fell down so that the view was blocked from the floor in front.

And then it happened.

Mrs. Joseph Mihelchich told authorities she was near the stage when she saw a man "all in black" up on the front of the stage among the children raise his hands and shout "Fire!"

Another woman on the stage said she heard a man speak in both Croatian and English shouting at least three times the word: "Fire!"

A 12-year-old girl named Annie would later tell how she saw a man with his back to her wave his hands and everybody rushed.

Whatever happened in those moments is unclear. But it sparked a tragedy that put Calumet onto the front pages of newspapers across the nation. The following days and weeks would bring a congressional investigation and involved lawyer Clarence Darrow and the muckraking journalist Upton Sinclair in a lobbying campaign for Gov. Ferris to take action on behalf of the miners.

On the stage, Anna Clemenc ran to the front and looked out into the hall. She said she saw a woman shaking a man by the shoulders but she saw no fire.

"Everything is OK! Sit down! Everything is OK!" she yelled.

But the panic could not be stopped.

As one, the great crowd turned toward the double doors at the back of the hall that led to the small platform and back down the 21 steps to the street. Faces full of panic, mouths open, chairs flying, screams and bedlam as mother's grabbed sons and father's grabbed daughters in a desperate effort to get out of the building.

News accounts speak of a father trying to protect his little daughter as the crowd surged over them. The daughter was crushed.

Auditorium doors opened onto a small platform and coat area before the six-foot wide stairs descended to an 6-by-10 foot foyer below. Double doors at the bottom of the stairs opened inward and double doors on the outside opened outward.

A woman picked up three children in her arms and tried to push back against the crowd at the top of the stairs. For a moment the crowd went backward and then surged forward

115

again. She lost her footing and fell, taking the children with her to their death.

A man braced his foot against the stair banister and with all his strength tried to stop the surge of the crowd, yelling: "Don't push! It's all right!"

The force of the crowd broke the banister and pushed him over the ledge to his and other's deaths.

More people started to tumble down the stairs. A Mrs. Aniemela was crushed as she stood upright trying to hold a baby above her head in the foyer.

Then as if they were pieces of human driftwood being swept over a waterfall, the bodies kept toppling one upon another. The staircase and foyer below filled with a mass of bodies. Screams arose from the pile and then muffled cries and then silence as the breathing stopped.

Those still alive slipped into shock. Moans and cries and in the auditorium scenes of shock and confusion and others heading down a fire escape at the side of the hall.

When firemen arrived they found a woman with two children standing on a cornice of the second-story window preparing to jump. Firemen prevented her from killing herself and the little ones by forcing her back through the window.

A girl jumped from the second-story but was caught by the fire chief who had just arrived. Another girl jumped and was caught by two boys. She and the boys just suffered bruises. An 18-year-old boy from Wolverine was given a baby to hold. He left by the fire escape and took it home. He found the child belonged to the family he boarded with. The baby's mother died in the crush.

Photo courtesy of Michigan Technological University Archives and Copper Country Historical Collections

The Italian Hall stairway that claimed 74 lives. Notice the two sets of doors, with the inner set opening inward.

Photo courtesy of Michigan Technological University Archives and Copper Country Historical Collections

The Italian Hall interior on Christmas Day, the morning after the disaster.

Photo courtesy of Michigan Technological University Archives and Copper Country Historical Collections

Mourners at a funeral service for some of the Italian Hall victims.

Some witnesses said rescuers could not open the doors from the street. They had to climb the fire escape and come at the mass of bodies from behind.

Others said the doors were open and the pile of bodies could be seen through the doorway.

What is known is that the only way rescuers could save anyone was climbing the fire escape on the south side of the building and entering the hall and running through the tumbled chairs to the stairway where they started pulling the living and dead out of the pile.

Some women saw rescuers come up the fire escape and thought they were anti-union thugs trying to harm them and rushed out the double doors and into the mass of people.

When rescuers entered the staircase a young 10-year-old girl cried for help. She was crushed against the wall by the mass of bodies. Two men tried to pull her out. Before they were able to release her, she died.

One boy who had fled the auditorium found himself waist-deep in bodies. Rescuers pulled him out. He went straight to the Catholic church where he was an altar boy. The priest tried to comfort him: "You poor, poor boy."

Some 70 years later he would stand in the village hall with tears streaming down his cheeks telling his story to Comptroller Susan Cone, still overcome.

One rescuer, Edward Manley, chief captain of the Waddell-Mahon detective agency of New York, pulled many people out of the mass but was injured himself in the crush. He suffered an injured back and internal injuries.

Bodies were pulled out of the jumbled hall of flesh. Child after child was dead. Then a mother holding her infant – both without life. Bodies were laid out on the sidewalk outside the hall.

Ethelyn Karinen and others would later remember the event at a special memorial service for victims of the disaster in 1989 and were quoted in the Calumet Daily Mining Gazette:

"We went there with my whole family. We went on a street car. We anticipated a very nice evening. When it happened, my mother was very calm. She said, "Don't move. There is no smoke. There is no fire.' So we listened to my mother.

"My mother helped revive one of the boys. When she got him revived, I remember very distinctly he had a nickel imbedded in his hand."

Another survivor who recounted his story at the memorial service was Frank Shaltz.

"I was lucky, I'll say that. I went down the steps and was squashed three or four steps from the bottom by all those people. I was trapped by my hips. Luckily, I was by the railing. I grabbed it and sort of eased myself up. Pat Ryan and my uncle each grabbed one of my arms but they couldn't pull me out."

Marry Webb said she was in the hall's kitchen.

"At the time someone shouted, 'Fire!' I was in the kitchen in back of the building. Someone had just opened a tub of maple chocolates. Someone grabbed me and put me on a ladder. There were all these people pushing me and shoving me, hitting me on the head with their shoes. I still don't know who put me on the ladder. I got down and ran down the alley, down Elm and home. I lost my coat, hat, overshoes, everything.

"I never did get any of those chocolates."

Mary Butina remembers the event as well.

121

"There was a big Christmas tree and we were all singing Christmas songs. All the little girls had dolls and all the boys had whistles. Then someone started yelling, 'Fire, Fire' and all those people were trying to get out. My mother took us down the fire escape to safety."

As the disaster unfolded, word spread though the mining villages of Red Jacket, Yellow Jacket and the others. Parents who sent their children to the hall alone came running. Mothers frantic and wailing ran up searching for the faces of their beloved ones.

Soon hundreds were there and police tried to form a line around the area to protect the injured and the dead bodies. But there was no stopping the hysterical mothers. Women frantically ran to the little figures on the sidewalk, wailing, searching, praying – hoping not to find their own little one.

Officials decided to move the bodies back inside the hall to prevent total chaos. So into the hall and the adjacent kitchen the bodies were laid, side-by-side. The Christmas tree remained on the stage – the season of hope suffocated by terror and one word: "Fire."

As the coroner examined body after body it became clear some died from crushed hearts and blood vessels, rather than suffocation. Those still alive were taken to nearby hospitals. The initial body count tallied 73 but on Christmas Day another person died as a result of injuries. In all fifty-six children, 13 women and five men were gone.

Word spread among the strikers that responsibility for the disaster rested with someone wearing a Citizen's Alliance button on his coat.

Mining company officials ordered their detective agency to begin searching for the man who mouthed the words. The president of the Western Federation of Miners, Charles H. Moyer, told reporters he sent a wire to President Woodrow Wilson asking for an investigation of the disaster.

"My information is that no strikers or anyone in sympathy with the strike brought about this catastrophe. There are many who testify that a man from the outside came up the stairs and yelled 'fire.'"

Moyer also told the press that the union would bury their own dead and did not want or need any help from the mining company or anyone else.

"No aid will be accepted from any of those citizens who a short time ago pronounced these people undesirable citizens," Moyer declared.

Some of the bodies were claimed by weeping mothers who took the bodies home and then realized it wasn't their child. They then brought the bodies back. Other women ran the streets calling for their little ones.

A grand jury, impaneled by the coroner, began searching for the truth of the disaster. Hearts softened among the city's non-mining population. Townspeople immediately began raising money to help the families. As news of the event arrived at telegraph offices and newspapers across the county, outrage swelled in the other mining regions.

On Christmas Day, instead of happy family gatherings and dinners, those with loved ones lost in the disaster mourned and prepared to bury their dead. A citizen's meeting in Calumet passed a resolution to try and put balm on the wounds of the bereaved.

"On the day which, throughout all Christendom is set aside as a day of rejoicing over the birth of the Savior, Calumet, stricken to the heart by an almost unbelievable catastrophe, stands mourning by the side of its dead. All bitterness and ill-feeling that has existed in this community during the past months is wiped away by one great common affliction. Today the people of Calumet can only see their neighbors, their brothers, their sisters, and their little children, staggering under an almost unbearable burden of distress and grief."

The resolution goes on:

"It is not for us today to try to ascertain the cause, nor to speculate as to how it might have been prevented. With feeble, mortal minds, we grope about in vain, we try to penetrate the evil which hides the logic and reason for the acts of God, and from the hearts of our people, the cry goes out today: 'Why must this overwhelming blow at this time strike a community and a people who have already suffered so much?' And there is no answer. We can only bow our heads and know that somewhere, some time and in His own good way, He himself will give the answer."

The resolution went on to form an assistance committee to help the suffering families in any way possible and to act as a mediator for contributions to the grieving families.

The coroner turned the Calumet Village Hall into a morgue, and Christmas Day many families went to the hall to receive the lifeless remains of their beloved. The local undertakers were overwhelmed by the tragedy and a train brought in 30 caskets and undertakers from Milwaukee to help prepare the bodies. Families came to the morgue and claimed bodies and took them home.

People of the city ignored Moyer's statements and donated freely to the cause. There was $7,000 collected in Red Jacket and Houghton raised $2,000 and donations were growing in other places.

The citizen's meeting appointed a committee to visit every stricken home and provide for funeral expenses and other needs.

Word came from the United Mine Workers, American Federation of Labor and other organizations of donations to be sent to the stricken families. The Western Federation of Miner's headquarters wired $5,000 from Denver for the needs.

Meanwhile, different descriptions of the man who shouted the word, "Fire" and different versions of where he came from and what he did afterward began to circulate in the community.

Some people at the hall said a man who wore a heavy beard opened the rear door of the hall and yelled, "Fire."

A woman in the hall, Mrs. Jacob Lustig, reported she sat beside the man inside the hall and he raised the alarm. She said he really did believe there was a blaze and ran from the room. She lost a child in the stampede.

Another witness told authorities that she saw a man rush for the exit with a boy whose cap was ablaze just before the stampede started.

A neighbor to the hall, Herman Bibber later would say he saw smoke rising from the hall at the time. And a check of one of the hall's chimneys later showed there was the possibility of a chimney fire.

The county prosecutor started a probe of the incident and Michigan Gov. Woodbridge Ferris appointed a special prosecutor, George E. Nichols, of Grand Rapids, to investigate as well.

Moyer told reporters he did not blame the Citizen's Alliance for the disaster.

"I do blame some of the rowdies and gunmen who have been in this district as mine guards and hired deputies for much of the violence that has occurred throughout the strike. But if such a catastrophe had occurred among the wives and children of members of the Citizen's Alliance, there would have been mob rule and possibly lynchings in the streets of Calumet."

Moyer received a telegram from Gov. Ferris that said simply: "All Michigan is in sorrow."

As President Woodrow Wilson spent the holiday in Pass Christian, Mississippi, government officials quietly informed the press that Moyer's demand for a federal investigation would likely go nowhere. Jurisdiction of the matter fell to the local authorities.

The next day, Dec. 26, witnessed a bizarre turn of events.

When the Citizen's Alliance women visited the stricken families homes, they refused to accept any assistance from the community.

Mining company spokesman A.F. Rees later would say the women received different responses in the homes.

"They would go to these places of suffering and sorrow, and those people would say, 'Yes, we need help. We want help. But we dare not take it. We are told that we must not take it.'

"In other places they were met with refusal, without any explanation of any kind. In other places they were actually insulted and driven away."

So the assistance committee asked for a meeting with Moyer. He agreed and they met at a hotel in Hancock. At the meeting, Moyer again declined to allow any assistance from the community to be given to the families. He also refused to recant his statement that the one who shouted "Fire" wore a Citizen's Alliance button on his overcoat.

The committee left.

A short time later, Moyer said he had visitors.

"I was beaten and attacked by about 25 men in my room at the Scott Hotel in Hancock last night. Struck on the head with the butt of a revolver, shot in the back and dragged through the hotel and streets and put on a train and told to leave that country forever," Moyer told reporters in Milwaukee as the train stopped on the way to Chicago. The reporters said Moyer was confined to his berth and the bed linen on the train was soiled with wounds from his scalp and back.

"At 8:30 o'clock last night Sheriff Cruse and about 15 other men came to my room to ask me about arrangement s for the burial of the poor persons who met their death in the Christmas catastrophe. They remained about 15 minutes and left after I had told them that the Western Federation of Miners and the labor organizations around the country could and would care for its own unfortunates.

"Within four minutes, before the committee of citizens could leave the hotel, 15 ruffians burst into the room. I was standing at the telephone at the time and was putting in a call. Charles H. Tanner, of California, traveling auditor for the Western Federation of Miners, was with me.

"Several grabbed hold of me and held me while another man came up from behind and struck me with the butt of his revolver on the head. Then there was a report of a gun and I felt a piercing sensation in my back. I do not think that anyone shot me deliberately. I think the gun used in hitting me on the head was discharged during the action."

Moyer described being taken to the train station where he alleged James McNaughton, the general manager of the mines warned him to never come back to Calumet or he would be hanged. McNaughton denied going to the train station and speaking to Moyer, saying he spent the evening with his wife and went to a social club.

Deputies allegedly handed tickets to the conductor for Moyer and Charles H. Tanner, auditor of the union, and rode with them to the Michigan line.

Once in Chicago, Moyer was taken to a hospital and his wounds were dressed.

As news of Moyer's deportation hit the newspapers, pressure on Gov. Ferris mounted. He ordered an inquiry into the events surrounding Moyer. Sheriff Cruce began the investigation.

As pressure mounted on Ferris, he sent a telegram to President Wilson, saying the state could handle the matter.

"I have notified President Wilson that so far as an investigation of the copper strike is concerned, we can look out for our own affairs without outside interference. I have been notified that a gentleman from the labor department will reach Lansing tonight."

On a cold, gray dreary Sunday, thousands of people, almost all the miners in the region, the citizens of Calumet and hundreds of others from across the Upper Peninsula and beyond gathered for the funeral procession from the six churches in the city where the bodies had been taken for final services.

Horse-drawn hearses lined up outside the doors of the churches and after the ceremonies, miners designated as pallbearers carried the caskets down to the waiting hearses. Some caskets were borne on shoulders of the men all the way to the cemetery.

A funeral procession some estimated at 50,000 people made its way down 5th Street to Pine Street and west about two miles Lakeview Cemetery.

Miners had taken pick axes and shovels to the winter-hardened cemetery ground and prepared graves for the caskets. One by one the boxes were laid into the graves and final words spoken.

Undoubtedly the incident gave incentive for both sides of the dispute to come up with a solution to solve the issues at hand.

As the bodies were placed in the graves, Moyer in his Chicago hospital bed took a turn for the worse. Meanwhile, the investigation into his deportation and the mining issues continued. Protests from labor organizations across the country became noisier as they demanded government intervention.

John Densmore, dispatched from Washington to investigate the matter for the Labor Department, arrived to try and talk with Gov. Ferris who was spending the holiday in his hometown of Big Rapids.

"I talked by telephone last night to Mr. Densmore when he was at Lansing and I asked him why he came," Ferris was quoted in the Detroit Free Press. "He replied that the department felt that the psychological moment, a fool phrase by the way, had arrived for action on the part of the government. Thereupon I left orders with my executive clerk to extend to Mr. Densmore all information at hand."

In a telegram from the Calumet sheriff, Ferris was informed the mining company chief was not involved in the deportation of

Moyer from the city. The governor put confidence in the grand jury investigation that the facts would be known.

Miners and socialists, however, said the grand jury would only back the mining company's views. Sen. James Martine, of New Jersey, wrote a letter to the Wilson Administration calling for an investigation.

"In view of the unfortunate labor troubles now and for many months existing in the copper mining districts of Michigan; and whereas, from reliable advices, I am informed that on Dec.26, President Charles H. Moyer of the Western Federation of Miners was forcibly abducted and carried out of the state of Michigan and it is currently stated that the abduction was advised, instigated, prompted and paid for by the mine owners or their representatives and in view of the fact that the Congress of the United States is not now in session and will not be until Jan. 12, 1914 ... As a citizen of the United States I respectfully pray that you appoint a special officer or officers to go promptly to the scene of that lawlessness and examine exhaustively into all conditions there now existing against peace and order."

In the end, U.S. Attorney General McReynolds ruled the issue was up to the state of Michigan. Gov. Ferris went to Calumet and met with miners and other officials.

The local grand jury ruled there was no evidence to prove the Citizen's Alliance was responsible for the disaster because of conflicting reports about the man who shouted "fire."

In February, a U.S. Congressional Delegation conducted a series of hearings held at Hancock City Hall into the mining dispute. The hearings are documented in "Conditions in Copper Mines of Michigan" a seven-volume document published by the House of Representatives Committee on Mines and Mining.

A.F. Rees representing the mining companies told investigators Moyer's decision to not accept help from the community hurt his cause and further opened wounds already evident in the hearts of everyone on both sides.

"Christmas Day was a day of mourning for everybody and everybody was filled with sympathy and a desire to help that ran through this whole country, this whole community. It was met by the statement of Mr. Moyer, rushed into the press of the entire country, where he refused to accept anything from the citizens of this country; and that horrible thing, that accident, was capitalized – there is no other word to express it."

Rees went on to testify that Moyer was fortunate to escape with his life.

Strikers went back to work in April 1914. But both sides lost. Company owners gave in to the demands for an eight-hour day. But the industry never really recovered and bitter feelings about it lingered as deep as some of the copper-ore veins below the city. Some strikers headed south to work in the auto plants; others went in search of mining jobs out West.

The Italian Hall disaster continued to stir hearts in the past century and into the new one. In the mid-1940s, balladeer Woodie Guthrie wrote a song about the Italian Hall disaster called the "1913 Massacre." The song takes the side of the miners and accuses the mine owners of being responsible for the incident.

And later in the century an opera about the disaster was staged and produced in Calumet.

As the new century begins, a documentary about the disaster and the impact of Woody Guthrie's song is now being put together by independent filmmakers Louis Galdieri and Ken Ross of New York City.

Galdieri heard about the incident through Arlo Guthrie's version of his father's song. He became so intrigued with the story, he made a trip to Calumet and uncovered a depth of emotion and feeling that remains 90 years later.

"This story has an entire existence. It's a whole subculture," Galdieri says.

The filmmakers were able to capture the thoughts of two survivors of the disaster and the last worker for the Calumet and Hecla Mining Co. Two of the three personalities tying the incident to the new century have now died. But their words live on among the 70 hours of footage already filmed for the documentary.

Titled "1913 Massacre" the documentary explores the impact of the incident on the current generation of those who live in Calumet and the impact of the song on American culture. The song has been recorded by Arlo Guthrie and was sung by Bob Dylan at Carnegie Hall in 1961.

"It was an incredible time," Ross says, listing the armed existence and the exploitation of miners and the focus on the copper mining industry by the rest of the world as America and other nations wired up for the electric light.

For many people, their only knowledge of the incident is through Guthrie's song. The filmmakers hope to keep the story alive because of its importance at many different levels.

"In a way, our film is a way of telling stories and passing them on," Ross says.

In Calumet, a monument now stands where the Italian Hall once stood. The hall was torn down in 1984. A memorial park on the site reminds visitors of the great loss of life and innocence that occurred on Christmas Eve 1913.

A search at the cemetery west of town reveals the graves of many of those who lost their lives. There are three sisters buried side by side with identical markers. There are many other stones recalling the names, the date of birth and the date of death as simply: "December 1913."

The graves of the three Klaric sisters who died in the Italian Hall tragedy in the cemetery outside Calumet.

The site of the Italian Hall is now a memorial park with the arch from the building that contained the doorway where so many died.

Chapter 10:
The Teen and the Tornado

Walls of wind, twisting wind -- a black monster wind -- swung its tail out of the sky. The huge weather ogre swooped out of its ambush, hungry for blood and destruction as it hit the ground just northwest of Flint and started vacuuming in the unsuspecting souls below.

It was 8:30 p.m. Monday, June 8, 1953. School ended the previous week for youngsters in the public school system. Summer vacation was under way.

In the still, muggy Michigan air some had gone swimming or biking or into the city for an outing and were returning.

135

Families were pulling into the drive-in theaters and buying popcorn waiting for the show to begin. But this night, the beautiful Michigan sunset disappeared behind the towering cumulous-nimbus giants on the horizon.

Already the nation had experienced devastating funnel clouds in Texas. During May, 15 tornadoes claimed 141 lives in Texas with much of the devastation centered at Waco. In all 227 Americans were dead because of tornadoes and the season was only beginning. The previous day, Sunday, tornadoes swept through Nebraska.

Now a storm system created by a cold front out of Wisconsin and a warm front from the Gulf of Mexico met over Michigan and made it a battleground – spitting out giant man killers in the process. Before the night was over tornadoes would claim 136 lives in Michigan and Ohio and the storm system later would spawn more killer whirlwinds in Massachusetts, taking 85 lives in Worcester.

In Flint, 116 would die, more than 800 would suffer injuries and 307 homes would be destroyed.

Scientists who classify funnel clouds labeled the Flint monster an F5 – the most powerful of tornadoes. That means its winds blew at 260 mph to 318 mph. Some believe this funnel cloud's winds reached 500 mph.

The counter-clockwise wind swinging into a house at that speed acted as a huge vacuum sucking everything up into its spinning torrent. Nothing could stand in its path. And as it arrived from west of Flint and set its sights on Coldwater Road in the Beecher District just one mile north of the city limits, all would feel its power.

Fred Shmidt, 15, earlier had walked home from swimming with his buddies and looked at the crazy sky to the west. He saw orange and purple and green clouds that seemed to be swirling and headed into a V-shaped dot on the horizon.

As he went into his house on Coldwater Road he found his mother already in her pajamas. She planned to go to bed early. His brother was playing with a neighbor boy and his young sister, Diane was playing near his mother.

They turned on the TV and then the electricity went out.

The monster stalking them would come with the darkness.

In other homes, mothers were preparing to put their young to bed while fathers labored on second shift at one of many General Motors plants. Some babysitters sat with their young charges while mothers and fathers enjoyed a few hours in Flint. Young men called on their sweethearts. Youngsters played hide-and-seek and the other games of summer.

Then the fist of wind and fury of nature swept down.

A farmer west of Coldwater Road was milking cows when his dog came in and bit the cow. The cow kicked the farmer. He grabbed the dog, spanked it and dragged it outside the barn. He looked up and saw the huge funnel coming his way. He ran to a low spot in the field and escaped.

The twister was huge – some one-half mile wide and it didn't seem to be in a hurry. Later estimates would clock its path at 15 mph as it slowly wreaked death and destruction in the manner of an ogre in a china shop.

At 1041 W. Coldwater Road, young Fred and his mother went to the window to see what was happening outside.

Branches, paper and other debris flew east down the street, not even touching the ground. They moved to the kitchen for a better view through their five-foot high by eight-foot wide picture window. The huge oak tree in front began rocking in the wind.

Then before their eyes, the immovable sentinel in their yard uprooted and fell on its side, sending dirt into the air. Its roots rose some six-feet out of the ground.

"Go lock the breezeway door," Fred's mom spoke with urgency.

Fred hurried through the kitchen toward the back of the house to the door that entered the breezeway.

"As I stood there, someone spoke to me in an audible voice – 'Don't go out there,'" Fred recalls. "My dad was at work and there was no one else in the room."

As he hesitated because of the voice, he heard the windows of the breezeway get pelted as if with BBs and then in an instant the breezeway was gone. He turned around and the south windows of the house burst allowing wind inside the house.

Swirling wind picked up anything not nailed down and made it a missile. Bricks and wood and paper flew through the kitchen. Fred became aware of things hitting him in the face but he felt no pain.

Instinctively he tried to get to the small entryway at the front door of the house. By now he was fighting the great strength of the wind. He leaped toward the entryway and landed. His brother was already there and his mom, holding his sister was trying to get there.

He reached up and pulled his mom down, covering her with his body.

The huge kitchen window bulged in an out with the pressure of the funnel.

"I was fascinated by it... I didn't understand how glass could do that," Fred says. Then it burst and instantly everything in the kitchen – the stove, refrigerator, china – vanished, sucked up into the huge cloud.

The roar of the monster became deafening as it took off the upper story of their house.

"Everything went black," Fred says. "And I woke up inside the funnel."

He remembers spinning around inside the huge funnel at least one and one-half times at great speed. The temperature inside the cloud was very hot.

"It felt like it was sucking my insides out, just turning me inside out."

With him inside were cars and houses and people. A huge load of 2-by-4 lumber just down the street had been sucked up by the cloud along with automobiles and homes.

Witnesses outside of the funnel who watched it from far off could see houses sucked up at the bottom and carried to the top where the funnel disappeared into the clouds. The houses looked like little toys.

The teenager blacked out after waking up inside the cloud and then "got spit out the back side" of the tornado on the ground some 50 yards from where his house used to be. He said he felt a tree or huge branch crash down on his leg and calf and then it was swept back up by the cloud.

"I was conscious for just a moment. I had to find out where mom was. It turned out I had a death grip on her. She was right there, bloody and torn and bruised over 100 percent of her body. The cartilage of her spine was injured and one toe was chopped off.

"I heard screaming ... way off in the distance I could hear my sister screaming and she was trying to crawl out of a pile of rubble, about two blocks away. She had her head split all across the top." She would later be sewed up.

His brother and a neighbor boy were off in another direction.

"The equivalent three or four blocks away my brother is picking up the neighbor boy. He is screaming at the top of his lungs. We thought his leg was broken but the guy got out of it without a broken bone. So did my brother. His back was all chopped up like mincemeat but he got out of it."

As for Fred, he became a victim of the monster. He believes he died as he lay back down and slipped into blackness.

"My back was chopped up, also my right leg broken, pulled apart about an inch, and a deep ditch (gash) down the back of my leg from the back of my knee down to my ankle. My ankle was crushed, my right foot was mangled to a pulp and I was a living pincushion. I looked like a porcupine. I had shivers of glass anywhere from four to six, seven-inches long sticking out of my body, all over my body. Everything, head, all over my body, there was not place I did not have it.

"Once I recognized this, a blackness just enshrouded me and I fell in heap and that was it. I knew I was dying and there was nothing I could do about it, I knew this was it."

He says he became unconscious and then his soul left his body and he started descending in a spiraling circle down into deep blackness and his surroundings started to become hot, unbearably hot as if in a furnace.

"I don't care if you believe it or not," he says. "It happened. You weren't there."

140

Being Jewish and not religious at all, the thought came to him: "Does hell really exist?

"I was straining my eyes to get my first eerie view of hell and it was like a blast furnace and suddenly for no explainable reason as if someone touched a button, I stopped. I lay there in that thick blackness totally unable to move.

"Suddenly as if someone else pushed a button, I began to go up. This time I was going straight up like on an elevator floor. And the longer it took, the more heat dissipated, it got cooler and cooler. I began to think, I wonder if I'm going to go back to the surface of the earth. I looked up and saw a transparent earth from underneath. I saw sightseers coming and saw the shattered Sunoco station on the corner of Coldwater and North Saginaw and the shattered Beecher Lumber Co.

"I was heading up toward a frame and I recognized my mom is standing over that frame, I recognized my brother and my sister and the neighbor boy is standing over that frame. The others are crying and calling to me, my mother especially and I recognized my body laying up there.

"And I know just as well when my soul entered back into that body and I ceased to be dead and was only unconscious – I knew the difference."

As the tornado passed by in its wake hail began to fall on the teen-ager's shredded back. He became conscious and his mother was screaming at him to move or he would be burned alive.

"When I was awake I made note that there was a wall of fire heading in my direction but it was too far away to feel. As I lay there I began to feel the heat of those flames. I started crawling away and I crawled away and all of a sudden the precise spot where I was laying shot up in a column of flame. A column

141

about three times higher than the trees had been before the tornado chopped them down. And then it settled into a flame about one and a half times the size of the trees."

What caused the flames?

"I was the only place and the only person of all the hundreds in the tornado that had landed on a broken gas main. And it burned and exploded all night long."

His mother encouraged him to get up and his brother brought a board for a crutch. The board broke under his weight. His mother and brother helped him up. The family was regathered and he began to walk with the glass and sticks and crushed ankle and broken leg toward the volunteer fire department building some three blocks away.

They saw three men approaching them.

"We thought they came to help us. We said, 'No we'll be all right, we're going to the Beecher Fire Dept. Go over and help the Whaleys they're buried in their basement we can hear their crying.' The men didn't say anything."

They watched as the men continued into the heart of the destruction and then the trio bent over to rob a body lying on the ground. Later they would learn police arrested the gruesome group.

When they reached the first street they found all the power lines down and wires creating an obstacle across it. Fred was going to try and crawl across them but his mother yelled out a warning.

"I don't care how much it hurts, you try and hop across and you don't hit a one." So with the help of his brother and neighbor he successfully hopped the wires on the road and fell into the ditch and passed out from the pain.

"The mercy of God!" he says. Later he would learn a neighbor stepped on a line and it blew his head off his shoulders.

They made two blocks and the teen passed out again. His mother could go no further. Some men arrived with a blanket as ambulances with lights flashing stopped outside the devastated area because of blocked streets and a mass of people running from all directions to gawk at the scene.

Men running into the carnage saw the group and carried his mother into a store and up to the second floor apartment. She would later go to the hospital. Later they came for Fred and put him in an ambulance and rushed him to Hurley Hospital. By the time he arrived, there was no room inside the hospital.

Mattresses had been put out on the lawn behind the ambulance barn and he was placed on one of the mattresses. More ambulance runs would bring more injured and dying.

As Fred lay there a man next to him kept rolling on top of his leg and causing him to pass out.

Later that night, men came and carried him to the 13th floor of the hospital and deposited him on a mattress on the floor. All around him were the wounded and dying. He then was taken down to the 12th floor outside the operating room where wives of members of the Beecher Fire Dept. found him and carefully washed the dirt and mud from between all the glass and wood sticking out of his body. He then was taken to the 11th floor and put into a bed.

He stayed there for another 24 hours. On Wednesday morning a man came to get him and take him to the operating room. When he arrived he found the doctors and nurses had been up and working for 36 hours straight. They were joking around. A doctor walked over to the gurney.

"The chief surgeon says don't mind us. We are doing all we can to stay awake. We're going to fix up that leg and set the thing and get you on the way to recovery."

One small problem, though, they had run out of anesthesia.

"I have nothing to deaden your pain. I have nothing to put you out with." They gave him a wooden tongue depressor to bite on and a black gentleman held his arms as one by one for the next 45 minutes the team pulled out the glass and wood from his body and cleaned him up, set his leg and ankle, sewed his calf and put a cast on it."

They took him back to his room and he fell asleep. He woke up at 2:30 a.m. with a nurse shaking him. She asked him if he was on the 13th floor of the hospital when he was brought in.

"Yes," Shmidt says. She checked his leg and ran out of the room. A short time later a whole medical team arrived.

"What's the problem?" Shmidt asked.

"There is a gangrene epidemic."

They got out the saw, took off the cast and found the disease already was eating at his leg.

"The doc said, 'Son we are going to do our best to save your leg. They operated right there. They scraped her and scraped her and gave me a gangrene shot. Anyway the next day I was popping out of the second cast."

They took that cast off and cleaned and scraped and again more shots and then the third cast stayed on."

It took three days for his father to find the family at the hospital. He'd been searching at the morgues and all the other places where bodies were. During the tornado he had been working as the projectionist at the Dort Drive-In Theater.

144

During Fred's stay in the hospital, his Jewish grandmother visited and brought a New Testament. She asked him to read it. She had taught him the kosher laws and now she asked him to read the New Testament. He read some of it as he lay for the rest of the time in the hospital.

"Oh, there was power in those words."

After 11 days, he and his mother were released. His brother and sister stayed just one day. As his father helped him into the family car both he and his mother started crying.

"It was something to walk outside and be hit with the smell of grass and the singing of birds. We got in the car and then they slammed the door shut. When they shut, it finally dawned on us that we were actually alive. Both of us broke down and we cried. Then they gave us a tour of the devastated way."

The family house was gone and in its place were two cars and parts of six other houses in the basement. His mother's mattress was in a tree and his dad's tackle box was found with all the metal lures fused together from the heat. Pieces of straw were stuck in trees as little arrows and there were many cars compacted in cubes against what was left of the Beecher Gymnasium wall.

Amazingly they found all of their canning jars intact in the basement and an unopened box of laundry soap perched on a beam.

Down the road near the GM factory, the tornado had taken the stacks of 2-by 4-inch framing material scooped from the lumberyard and drove each piece in the ground along the rocky railroad grade at a 45-degree angle.

"It set them like a picket fence."

Busses from the high school were carried six miles away and put into fields. An I-beam from the gymnasium at Beecher High School was stripped off the building and carried a mile and dropped on a GM factory.

They learned of an elderly neighbor who had been in bed when the storm hit was taken into the funnel, bed and all, and gently put down in the field. Another set of neighbors, a divorcee and her children all died.

Tragic stories were many. A Coldwater Street neighbor working at an auto plant lost his entire family. Their next-door neighbors lost their father and the rest of the family all were injured.

"I lost a lot of friends that day," Shmidt says.

Witnesses compared the aftermath of the tornado to the result of an atomic bomb or something similar.

A Lansing State Journal reporter, Frank Hand, described it this way: "Bombs would have been more merciful – something would have been left standing. Here nothing – not one man-made thing was left. The few trees that were left standing were so badly beaten by parts of buildings and cars thrown against them they probably will have to be cut down."

Three off-duty Detroit police officers were arrested for looting a damaged home. But the good actions of others outweighed the bad.

Firefighters and ambulance crews drove themselves through the night searching for the living amid the rubble. Physicians in the hospitals around the area spent two or three sleepless days donating their services to victims.

The twister robbed the utility companies.

Consumers Power needed to fix 70 miles of electric line and install 200 poles and Michigan Bell lost 400 utility poles and nine miles of line. The Beecher water tower escaped the tornado but when workers checked its catwalk, 100 feet above the ground, they found a doll laying on it.

Gov. G. Mennen Williams rushed to the disaster scene from an engagement in Bay City and helped coordinate rescue efforts. More than 500 National Guard troops and 150 state police from around the state arrived to help with rescue efforts and provide security to the damaged area.

In addition to Flint, the tornado brought destruction and injuries to the Port Huron area and another tornado near Tawas killed four people while a third tornado near Erie claimed four lives.

Relief efforts from the state and community were immediate. And Beecher, which was not part of the city of Flint, began to clean up and rebuild its infrastructure. By August a massive volunteer effort was under way to rebuild the destroyed homes.

Both General Motors and the United Auto Workers union gave generously to a relief fund that was added to by hundreds of others.

An Indiana congressman asked for an investigation into the link between atomic bomb testing in Nevada and the deadly outbreak of tornadoes across the nation. Rep. Madden theorized that because of the radioactivity entering the atmosphere, it could generate "abnormal atmospheric conditions" and produce tornadoes.

The National Weather Service quickly zapped his theory. They blamed the fact that tornadoes were hitting populated areas

147

and not the countryside where less lives and damage would occur.

The Flint-Beecher Tornado is recognized as the last tornado in the U.S. to claim more than 100 lives. It is rated as the ninth deadliest funnel cloud in U.S. history.

President Eisenhower, in the state on other business a week later, witnessed the destruction in a flyover and sent a message to the victims.

"Even a fleeting look at the destroyed section of your city, such as we were able to obtain as we flew over it today, clearly shows the destructive force of a tornado and the extent of the disaster suffered by many of your citizens. My sympathies and best wishes go to each of those families."

For Shmidt, the tornado changed his life.

"It was positively the turning point," he says. "It awakened me to my spiritual need to find God."

As a non-religious Jew he began to seek out God. He started attending a church and two years later he met a young lady working at a drive-in restaurant who invited him to church with her. He went and saw something there that he knew to be real and that he didn't have at the church he was attending.

As he listened to a message preached, he understood his need to repent before God of his sins. He went to an altar and confessed his sins and gave himself to the Jesus Christ and a short time later received the Holy Spirit. He spoke in another language, just as the apostles did in the Book of Acts in the Bible.

His family disowned him for a time, but later came to the same faith he had. Fred married the girl who invited him to church. Her name is Darlene.

Two years later God called him into the ministry and he has since pastored and preached around the world and now has an international prophecy and teaching ministry centered in Powhatan, Virginia. He travels to Israel often and shares with other Jews that Jesus is the messiah.

He's appeared on Christian TV and radio programs.

When he looks back at the tornado and how he could have died and his experience of death as he felt his soul leave his body, he has one phrase that is often repeated.

"Oh, the mercy of God."